History's Cultural Impact

Erasing Minority Contributions

Alex Hasten

ISBN: 978-1-77961-353-0
Imprint: Telephasic Workshop

Contents

Introduction

The Importance of Minority Contributions in History

Recognizing the Diverse Mosaic of Humanity

In order to understand the importance of minority contributions in history, it is crucial to recognize the diverse mosaic of humanity. Throughout the ages, civilizations have flourished and developed across the world, each with its own unique characteristics, traditions, and innovations. Unfortunately, traditional historical narratives have often overlooked or marginalized the contributions of minority groups, leading to skewed perceptions of history. It is imperative that we reevaluate these perspectives and acknowledge the rich and varied tapestry of human experiences.

The Complexity of Human Cultures

Human cultures are intricate and multifaceted, shaped by a variety of factors such as geography, climate, resources, and historical events. This diversity is evident in the vast array of languages, customs, arts, music, and technologies that have emerged throughout history. Each culture brings its own perspective, knowledge, and values, enriching the global collective heritage. By recognizing the diverse mosaic of humanity, we can develop a more comprehensive understanding of the world and appreciate the interconnectedness of different cultures.

Challenging Eurocentric Perspectives

Eurocentrism, the viewpoint that prioritizes European history and culture over others, has long been pervasive in historical narratives. This perspective has often overshadowed or undermined the contributions of minority groups, creating a distorted representation of history. By examining history from a global perspective and recognizing the contributions of diverse cultures, we challenge the Eurocentric bias and create a more inclusive and accurate account of human achievements.

Valuing Indigenous and Traditional Knowledge

Indigenous peoples have a deep understanding of their environments and have developed complex systems of knowledge that sustainably utilize natural resources. Their traditional ecological knowledge, passed down through generations, holds invaluable insights into land management, agriculture, medicine, and sustainable practices. By recognizing and valuing their contributions, we can learn from their wisdom and work towards a more sustainable future.

Promoting Inclusivity and Representation

Ignoring minority contributions in history perpetuates systemic biases and perpetuates inequality. By redefining historical narratives to include the experiences and accomplishments of diverse groups, we promote inclusivity and representation. This recognition not only gives voice to marginalized communities but also creates a more accurate and comprehensive understanding of the human experience.

Consequences of Ignoring Minority Contributions

The neglect of minority contributions in history has far-reaching consequences. It perpetuates stereotypes, reinforces prejudices, and marginalizes already underrepresented groups. In addition, it limits our understanding of the full extent of human potential, hindering our ability to address current societal challenges. By acknowledging and celebrating the contributions of minority groups, we create a more inclusive and just society.

Unearthing Hidden Histories

Recognizing the diverse mosaic of humanity involves unearthing hidden histories that have been forgotten, suppressed, or intentionally erased. This process requires diligent research, collaboration with communities, and the inclusion of multiple perspectives. By shedding light on these hidden histories, we uncover valuable insights and restore the voices and contributions of those who have been silenced.

Summary

Recognizing the diverse mosaic of humanity is essential to understanding the true richness and complexity of human history. Challenging Eurocentric perspectives, valuing indigenous and traditional knowledge, promoting inclusivity and representation, and unearthing hidden histories are all crucial steps towards creating a more accurate and inclusive narrative. By doing so, we honor the contributions of all cultures and pave the way for a better future built upon diversity and understanding. It is our responsibility to ensure that history reflects the diversity of human experiences and acts as a source of inspiration for generations to come.

Redefining the Narrative of History

In the study of history, it is fundamental to examine the perspective from which historical events and figures are portrayed. The dominant narratives throughout history have often marginalized and underrepresented the contributions of minority groups, such as indigenous peoples, women, LGBTQ+ individuals, and religious minorities. This section aims to shed light on the need for redefining the narrative of history by acknowledging and celebrating the significant roles played by these underrepresented groups.

Understanding Historical Bias

Before diving into the redefinition of history, it is crucial to recognize the existence of historical bias. Historians and scholars have traditionally focused on the achievements and contributions of those in positions of power and authority. As a result, the stories and experiences of minority groups have been overlooked or intentionally excluded from historical accounts. This bias perpetuates a limited view of history and hinders a comprehensive understanding of human achievements and progress.

Embracing a Diverse Perspective

Redefining the narrative of history entails embracing a more diverse and inclusive perspective. This involves actively seeking out the stories, voices, and experiences of individuals and communities who have historically been sidelined. By doing so, we can gain a more holistic understanding of the past and appreciate the multifaceted nature of human civilization.

Challenging Eurocentrism

One prominent aspect of the traditional historical narrative is its Eurocentrism—the tendency to prioritize European perspectives and contributions while neglecting those from other regions of the world. To redefine the narrative of history, it is essential to challenge and dismantle Eurocentric biases. This can be achieved by giving equal importance to non-European civilizations, including their scientific advancements, cultural achievements, and societal contributions.

Unveiling Hidden Figures

Redefining the narrative of history involves uncovering the stories and achievements of individuals who have been erased or forgotten. This requires diligent research and exploration, often through archival work or oral history projects. By bringing these hidden figures to the forefront, we enrich our understanding of history and ensure that their contributions are properly recognized and celebrated.

Promoting Intersectionality

An important aspect of redefining the narrative of history is recognizing the interconnectedness of identities and experiences. Intersectionality acknowledges that individuals have multiple, overlapping social identities, such as race, gender, and sexual orientation, which shape their unique experiences and perspectives. By promoting an intersectional approach to studying history, we can gain a more nuanced understanding of the diverse contributions made by individuals across different marginalized communities.

Reevaluating Historical Interpretations

To truly redefine the narrative of history, we must critically reevaluate existing historical interpretations and reinterpret events and figures through a more inclusive lens. This involves questioning prevailing narratives, challenging assumptions, and embracing alternative perspectives. By doing so, we contribute to a more accurate and comprehensive understanding of history.

Teaching the Redefined Narrative

Finally, the redefined narrative of history must be incorporated into educational curricula and disseminated widely. We must ensure that future generations learn about the diverse contributions of minority groups, and understand the historical context and significance of these contributions. By teaching a more inclusive history, we can foster empathy, understanding, and respect for all cultures and communities.

In conclusion, redefining the narrative of history is a vital undertaking that seeks to acknowledge and celebrate the contributions of minority groups. By embracing a diverse perspective, challenging biases, uncovering hidden figures, promoting intersectionality, reevaluating interpretations, and integrating a redefined narrative into education, we can create a more inclusive and accurate understanding of the past. This comprehensive approach to history allows us to appreciate the complexity of human achievements and honors the vast mosaic of diverse cultures and identities.

Challenging Traditional Historical Perspectives

In the study of history, it is crucial to question and challenge traditional historical perspectives. These perspectives have often been shaped by dominant cultures and majority narratives, resulting in the erasure or marginalization of minority contributions. Challenging these perspectives is essential as it allows for a more accurate and inclusive understanding of the past, bringing to light the significant contributions made by historically marginalized groups.

One way to challenge traditional historical perspectives is by examining the bias inherent in primary sources. Primary sources, such as documents, artifacts, and eyewitness accounts, are valuable resources for historians. However, they can reflect the biases of the individuals who created or preserved them. For example, historical accounts written by colonizers or conquerors tend to highlight their achievements while downplaying or ignoring the contributions of the colonized or conquered societies. By critically analyzing these primary sources, historians can uncover the hidden narratives and recover the lost voices of marginalized communities.

Another approach to challenging traditional historical perspectives is through the exploration of alternative sources of knowledge. Traditional historical accounts often prioritize written records and official documents, neglecting the valuable oral traditions, folklore, and cultural expressions of marginalized groups. By incorporating diverse sources of knowledge, such as oral histories or songs, historians can gain a more comprehensive understanding of the experiences and contributions of minority communities. These alternative sources can enrich our understanding of the past and challenge the dominant narratives that have overshadowed minority contributions.

Furthermore, it is essential to question the interpretation and framing of historical events. Historians must critically examine the frameworks through which historical events are analyzed and interpreted. The lens through which we view history can influence the significance and visibility of minority contributions. For instance, a Eurocentric perspective may prioritize European achievements, relegating the contributions of indigenous peoples or other marginalized groups to the periphery. By adopting a more inclusive and intersectional approach, historians can challenge these biases and provide a more accurate representation of historical events.

Challenging traditional historical perspectives also involves acknowledging the role of power dynamics in shaping historical narratives. Power structures, including colonialism, patriarchy, and racism, have influenced historical interpretations and marginalized certain individuals or groups. By recognizing these power dynamics, historians can confront the biases and inequalities that have shaped historical perspectives. This understanding can help uncover the hidden stories and contributions of minority communities and bring about a more equitable representation of history.

In the quest to challenge traditional historical perspectives, it is important to engage in ongoing dialogue and collaboration with diverse communities. Historians should actively seek out perspectives from individuals and communities whose stories have been marginalized or excluded from dominant narratives. This collaborative approach ensures that the history being written is more inclusive, accurate, and representative of the diverse mosaic of humanity.

To illustrate the importance of challenging traditional historical perspectives, let us consider the case of Rosalind Franklin, a scientist whose contributions to the discovery of the structure of DNA were overshadowed for many years. Franklin's work was critical in providing evidence for the double helix structure of DNA, yet her contributions were downplayed and often attributed solely to her male colleagues, James Watson and Francis Crick. It was only later that Franklin's crucial role was recognized, highlighting the significance of challenging traditional perspectives in acknowledging the contributions of marginalized individuals.

In conclusion, challenging traditional historical perspectives is essential for recognizing the contributions of marginalized communities throughout history. By critically analyzing primary sources, exploring alternative sources of knowledge, questioning interpretations, acknowledging power dynamics, and engaging in collaboration, historians can create a more accurate and inclusive understanding of the past. Challenging these perspectives not only enriches our knowledge of history but also contributes to a more just and equitable society.

Impact on Identity and Cultural Heritage

Understanding the impact of minority contributions in history goes beyond the recognition of their achievements. It extends into the realm of identity and cultural heritage. The contributions of minority groups shape our collective identity, enrich our understanding of humanity, and strengthen the cultural fabric of societies. In this section, we will explore how minority contributions impact individual and collective identities, as well as cultural heritage.

Identity Formation

The recognition and inclusion of minority contributions in history help individuals develop a more nuanced understanding of their own identity. When individuals realize that their cultural, ethnic, or social background has contributed significantly to the broader narrative of history, it instills a sense of pride and belonging. This acknowledgment becomes a source of empowerment and affirmation, enabling individuals to embrace their heritage and cultural identity with confidence.

For example, when Indigenous peoples learn about the vast contributions of their ancestors to science, medicine, agriculture, and art, it strengthens their connection to their roots. It reinforces their unique cultural identity and provides a foundation for self-esteem and personal growth. Similarly, when LGBTQ+ individuals discover the impactful contributions made by LGBTQ+ historical figures, artists, and activists, they find inspiration and courage to embrace their identity unapologetically.

Cultural Heritage Preservation

Minority contributions in history play a crucial role in preserving and promoting cultural heritage. By recognizing and celebrating the achievements and practices of diverse communities, we ensure the survival of their rich cultural traditions for future generations. Cultural heritage encompasses the tangible and intangible aspects of a community's identity, including language, rituals, music, dance, art, and cuisine.

When we acknowledge the contributions of African and African American communities, for instance, it not only recognizes their impact on history but also helps to preserve their cultural heritage. From ancient African civilizations to the influence of African American culture in the United States, these contributions have profoundly shaped art, music, literature, and social movements. By documenting and showcasing these contributions, we ensure the preservation and continuation of their cultural traditions.

Promoting Inclusion and Empathy

By highlighting minority contributions in history, we foster a greater sense of inclusion and empathy within society. Understanding the struggles, achievements, and cultural heritage of minority communities encourages respect and appreciation for diverse perspectives. This, in turn, leads to a more equitable and harmonious society that values the richness and complexity of human experience.

For instance, when we learn about the contributions of women throughout history, we challenge the patriarchal narratives that have historically marginalized their achievements. Recognizing the instrumental roles women have played in social movements, sciences, arts, and literature promotes gender equality and fosters empathy towards their experiences. It allows for a more comprehensive understanding of history and encourages the empowerment of women in contemporary society.

Uncovering Hidden Narratives

The inclusion of minority contributions in history helps to uncover hidden narratives that have been overshadowed or erased by dominant historical perspectives. These hidden narratives expose the biases and limitations in traditional historical accounts, providing a more accurate and comprehensive understanding of the past.

For example, the chapter on immigrant contributions and cultural exchange sheds light on the significant influence of Asian immigrants and European immigrants on American society. These contributions have often been neglected or downplayed in mainstream historical narratives. By unearthing these hidden narratives, we challenge misconceptions, promote intercultural understanding, and acknowledge the diverse contributions that have shaped our societies.

Caveats and Challenges

While recognizing and documenting minority contributions in history is essential, it is crucial to approach this task with care. It requires diligent research, sensitivity, and a commitment to inclusivity. We must be mindful of inadvertently reducing complex historical narratives to a singular perspective or reinforcing stereotypes. The intent should be to amplify and celebrate the diverse array of contributions, rather than tokenize or essentialize minority groups. It is also important to recognize the limitations of available historical records and the challenges of reconstructing marginalized histories. By acknowledging these caveats and challenges, we ensure a more nuanced and accurate portrayal of minority contributions and their impact on identity and cultural heritage.

Summary

In this section, we explored the impact of minority contributions on identity and cultural heritage. We discussed how the recognition of such contributions fosters personal and collective identity formation, preserves cultural heritage, promotes inclusion and empathy, and uncovers hidden narratives. While acknowledging the importance of minority contributions, we also highlighted the need for careful research, sensitivity, and a commitment to inclusivity in presenting and celebrating these contributions. By embracing the full spectrum of human experiences and narratives, we enrich our understanding of history and foster a more equitable and empowered society.

Consequences of Ignoring Minority Contributions

Ignoring the contributions of minority groups in history has far-reaching consequences that impact our understanding of the world and its diverse cultures. By neglecting the achievements and experiences of these marginalized communities, we not only perpetuate an incomplete narrative but also reinforce existing power dynamics and inequalities. In this section, we will explore some of the consequences of ignoring minority contributions, highlighting the importance of recognizing and celebrating the diversity of human history.

Misrepresentation and Incomplete Historical Narratives

One of the primary consequences of neglecting minority contributions is the perpetuation of misrepresentation and incomplete historical narratives. Traditional historical accounts have often centered around the achievements of dominant groups, marginalizing the experiences and accomplishments of others. This skewed representation distorts our understanding of the past, painting an incomplete picture of human history.

For example, many textbooks have overlooked or downplayed the influence of indigenous cultures on scientific advancements, agricultural practices, and mathematical knowledge. By neglecting to effectively convey the rich indigenous contributions, we deny students the opportunity to appreciate and learn from these valuable insights. This not only perpetuates stereotypes and biases but also hinders our understanding of scientific and cultural progress.

Reinforcement of Power Dynamics

Ignoring minority contributions reinforces existing power dynamics and perpetuates social inequalities. Throughout history, dominant groups have often controlled the production and dissemination of knowledge, prioritizing their own perspectives and experiences. This exclusionary approach reinforces the marginalization of minority communities and maintains the status quo.

By excluding the contributions of women, for instance, we reinforce the systemic gender inequalities that have persisted for centuries. Women have played vital roles in social movements, scientific advancements, and artistic expressions, yet their contributions have been overshadowed or ignored. This perpetuates the notion that women's voices and experiences are somehow less important, leading to continued marginalization and underrepresentation.

Negative Impact on Identity and Cultural Heritage

The omission of minority contributions can have a negative impact on the identity and cultural heritage of marginalized communities. When history neglects the achievements and struggles of these groups, it denies them a sense of belonging and validation, further eroding their sense of self-worth.

For example, by overlooking the rich cultural and artistic traditions of Indigenous peoples, we contribute to the erasure of their identity. This erasure not only dismisses the value of Indigenous heritage but also fuels cultural assimilation, further marginalizing these communities.

Narrowed Perspectives and Missed Opportunities

By ignoring the contributions of minority groups, we limit our perspectives and miss out on valuable opportunities for growth and progress. History is a collective story that encompasses the experiences and achievements of diverse peoples. When we exclude certain voices and narratives, we deny ourselves the chance to learn from different perspectives and expand our understanding of the world.

For instance, LGBTQ+ contributions in various fields, such as literature, art, and activism, have played a significant role in shaping society. By neglecting to highlight these contributions, we limit our understanding of human potential and miss out on opportunities for social and cultural advancement.

Impact on Education and Empathy

The omission of minority contributions in educational curricula has a direct impact on students' education and empathy. When students are not exposed to diverse perspectives and histories, they are limited in their capacity to understand, respect, and empathize with others.

By integrating minority contributions into educational materials, we broaden students' understanding of the world and encourage empathy towards marginalized communities. This helps foster a more inclusive society and equips students with the knowledge and tools needed to challenge stereotypes and discrimination.

In conclusion, ignoring minority contributions in history has significant consequences that extend far beyond the pages of textbooks. By perpetuating misrepresentation, reinforcing power dynamics, and limiting perspectives, we hinder progress towards a more inclusive and equitable society. Recognizing and celebrating the diverse mosaic of humanity is not only a matter of justice and respect but also a crucial step towards a more comprehensive understanding of history and the world we live in.

Chapter 1: The Role of Indigenous Peoples

Section 1: Indigenous Innovations and Knowledge Systems

Subsection 1: Indigenous Science and Medicine

Indigenous communities around the world have developed remarkable knowledge systems in the fields of science and medicine, which have contributed to the well-being of their communities for centuries. In this subsection, we will explore some of the key aspects of Indigenous science and medicine, highlighting their unique perspectives and contributions.

Traditional Healing Practices

Indigenous cultures have always placed a strong emphasis on maintaining holistic well-being and understanding the interconnectedness of the human body, mind, and spirit. Traditional healing practices reflect this comprehensive approach by addressing not only physical ailments but also emotional, mental, and spiritual imbalances.

For example, among Native American tribes, traditional healers, known as medicine people or shamans, use herbs, rituals, and spiritual practices to facilitate healing. These practices often involve an understanding of the balance between humans and nature, the use of sacred plants, and the belief that illness can stem from a disruption in one's relationship with the natural world.

Ethnobotany and Medicinal Plants

Indigenous communities have an extensive knowledge of the natural environment and the medicinal properties of plants. This knowledge is often passed down through generations and plays a crucial role in their healthcare systems.

Ethnobotany is the study of the traditional knowledge and usage of plants by indigenous peoples. It involves identifying and documenting the medicinal properties of various plant species and the methods of preparation and administration. Indigenous healers have in-depth knowledge of the pharmacological qualities of plants and use them to treat a wide range of ailments.

For example, the Quechua people in the Andean region of South America have long used the coca plant for medicinal purposes. Coca leaves contain alkaloids such as cocaine and are considered a powerful stimulant, pain reliever, and digestive aid. However, the traditional use of coca leaves is far removed from the extraction and synthesis of cocaine, which has led to its misuse and prohibition.

Traditional Ecological Knowledge (TEK)

Indigenous cultures have a profound understanding of their local ecosystems and have developed sustainable practices based on this knowledge. Traditional Ecological Knowledge (TEK) encompasses not only the scientific understanding of ecosystems but also the cultural, spiritual, and ethical aspects of human-nature relationships.

TEK includes a deep understanding of ecological patterns, animal behavior, weather patterns, and the interactions between species. Indigenous communities have developed ecologically sustainable practices, such as rotational farming, agroforestry, and ecosystem-based fisheries management, which have allowed them to thrive in harmony with nature for millennia.

One example of TEK is the land management techniques employed by the Indigenous peoples of Australia. The practice of "firestick farming" involves controlled burning of the landscape to promote the regrowth of certain plant species and manage the impacts of wildfires. This not only helps maintain biodiversity but also enhances the productivity of the land for hunting, gathering, and agriculture.

Indigenous Astronomy and Mathematics

Indigenous cultures have a rich tradition of studying the night sky and developing sophisticated astronomical knowledge and mathematical systems. Rather than viewing the cosmos as separate from human existence, Indigenous cosmologies often integrate celestial observations into their cultural and spiritual practices.

For example, the Maori people of New Zealand have a deep understanding of the stars and their movements, which they use for navigation, calendar keeping, and storytelling. The star cluster known as the Pleiades, or Matariki in Maori, is a significant marker of the Māori New Year and a time for community celebration.

Indigenous mathematical systems also differ from the Eurocentric approach, with unique numbering systems and geometric principles. The Mayans, for instance, developed a highly advanced numerical system that included the concept of zero and precise astronomical calendars.

Preserving Indigenous Knowledge

Despite the rich contributions of Indigenous science and medicine, much of this knowledge has been marginalized, suppressed, or appropriated by Western scientific frameworks. It is crucial to recognize and respect the intellectual property rights and cultural sovereignty of Indigenous communities.

Efforts are being made to bridge the gap between traditional Indigenous knowledge and mainstream science by promoting collaboration, inclusion, and the elevation of Indigenous voices. Furthermore, the protection and revitalization of Indigenous languages, which serve as vessels of traditional knowledge, are of utmost importance.

In conclusion, Indigenous science and medicine present unique perspectives and knowledge systems that have significant contributions to make in the broader understanding of human well-being and the environment. By recognizing and respecting Indigenous knowledge, we can enrich our collective understanding of science, medicine, and the world around us.

Subsection 2: Sustainable Agricultural Practices

In this subsection, we will explore the concept of sustainable agricultural practices and their importance in promoting environmental conservation and ensuring food security. Sustainable agriculture is an approach to farming that aims to meet the needs of the present generation without compromising the ability of future generations to meet their own needs. It emphasizes the use of environmentally friendly practices, resource conservation, and the promotion of biodiversity.

Principles of Sustainable Agriculture

Sustainable agriculture is guided by several key principles that help farmers minimize negative environmental impacts and improve long-term productivity. These principles include:

1. Conservation of natural resources: Farmers should strive to protect and conserve soil, water, and air quality. This can be achieved through practices such as crop rotation, cover cropping, and the use of conservation tillage techniques.
2. Biodiversity promotion: Encouraging biodiversity on farms is crucial for maintaining healthy ecosystems. This can be achieved by incorporating diverse crops, creating wildlife habitats, and implementing integrated pest management strategies.
3. Waste reduction and recycling: Minimizing waste production and reusing valuable resources is essential in sustainable agriculture. Composting, recycling of organic matter, and reducing chemical inputs can significantly reduce the environmental impact of farming.
4. Minimizing chemical inputs: Sustainable agriculture promotes the reduced use of synthetic pesticides and fertilizers. Instead, farmers are encouraged to use organic and biological pest control methods, nutrient management techniques, and natural soil amendments.

Challenges and Solutions

Implementing sustainable agricultural practices can pose challenges for farmers. However, these challenges have practical solutions that can be adopted to overcome them. Let's explore some common challenges and their corresponding solutions:

1. Soil erosion: Excessive soil erosion can degrade soil quality and reduce productivity. To combat this, farmers can implement soil conservation practices such as contour plowing, terracing, and the use of windbreaks.
2. Water scarcity: In regions with limited water resources, farmers can adopt water-efficient irrigation systems like drip irrigation or precision sprinklers. Additionally, collecting rainwater and recycling wastewater can help decrease water demand.
3. Pest and disease management: Sustainable agriculture promotes the use of integrated pest management (IPM) strategies. IPM involves a combination of cultural, biological, and chemical control methods to manage pests and diseases effectively. These methods include crop rotation, biological control agents, and targeted pesticide application.

4. Soil fertility maintenance: Continuous cropping can lead to nutrient depletion in the soil. To address this, farmers can incorporate organic matter through cover cropping, composting, and the use of animal manure. Additionally, using precise nutrient management techniques can ensure optimal soil fertility.

Case Study: Permaculture Farming

Permaculture is an innovative approach to sustainable agriculture that aims to create self-sufficient ecosystems modeled after natural ecosystems. It combines principles of sustainable design and ecological principles to develop food-producing systems that are both productive and environmentally friendly.

Permaculture farming emphasizes the following practices:

1. Agroforestry: Integrating woody perennials like fruit trees and nitrogen-fixing plants into the farm system enhances biodiversity, provides shade, and prevents soil erosion.

2. Polyculture: Growing a diverse range of crops together promotes natural pest control, reduces disease risk, and maximizes resource utilization.

3. Water management: Implementing techniques such as swales, ponds, and rainwater harvesting systems helps store and manage water efficiently, reducing water waste and enhancing water availability during dry periods.

4. Natural pest control: Attracting beneficial insects, birds, and other animals through the creation of diverse habitats helps control pests naturally.

Permaculture farming demonstrates the potential of sustainable agricultural practices in creating resilient and productive farming systems.

Conclusion

Sustainable agricultural practices play a crucial role in ensuring long-term food security, environmental conservation, and the well-being of future generations. By embracing principles such as resource conservation, biodiversity promotion, waste reduction, and minimal chemical inputs, farmers can mitigate the negative impacts of conventional farming practices. Addressing challenges through solutions like soil conservation, water-efficient irrigation, integrated pest management, and soil fertility maintenance will pave the way for a sustainable and resilient agricultural sector. The case study on permaculture farming highlights the potential of innovative approaches in achieving sustainable food production. It is essential for agricultural systems worldwide to embrace sustainable practices to create a healthier and more sustainable future for all.

Subsection 3: Traditional Ecological Knowledge

Traditional Ecological Knowledge (TEK) refers to the wisdom and understanding that indigenous communities have acquired over generations about their environment. It encompasses the intimate relationship between humans and nature, highlighting the interconnectedness and interdependence of all living beings. In this subsection, we will explore the significance of TEK, its principles, and its contributions to sustainable ecosystems.

The Principles of Traditional Ecological Knowledge

TEK is based on various fundamental principles that guide indigenous communities' understanding and interaction with their natural surroundings. These principles are deeply rooted in their cultural heritage and provide valuable insights into environmental stewardship. Let's explore some of these principles:

1. **Holism and interconnectedness:** Indigenous cultures perceive the Earth as a complex web of interconnected relationships. They recognize that every component of the ecosystem, ranging from plants and animals to rivers and mountains, plays a vital role in maintaining balance and harmony. This holistic perspective guides their conservation efforts, promoting the protection of the entire ecosystem rather than focusing solely on individual species or resources.

2. **Sustainability:** Indigenous communities have long understood the importance of sustainable resource use. They recognize that the Earth's resources are finite and must be managed carefully to ensure their availability for future generations. Through practices such as selective harvesting, rotational farming, and habitat restoration, they maintain equilibrium between human needs and nature's capacity to regenerate.

3. **Adaptation and resilience:** Indigenous knowledge systems recognize the dynamic nature of ecosystems and the need for adaptation to changing environmental conditions. Over centuries, indigenous communities have developed strategies to cope with natural disturbances like floods, droughts, and wildfires. These strategies often involve flexible land-use practices, diversified agricultural systems, and the preservation of biodiversity as a buffer against environmental uncertainties.

4. **Place-based knowledge:** Indigenous cultures have an intimate connection with their ancestral lands. They possess a deep understanding of local

ecosystems, including the behavior of wildlife, the life cycles of plants, and the changing seasons. This ecological knowledge is passed down through generations, allowing communities to make informed decisions about land use, resource management, and conservation measures that are specific to their unique environments.

These principles, woven into the fabric of traditional ecological knowledge, offer valuable lessons for our modern society in achieving sustainable and resilient ecosystems. By recognizing the importance of these principles, we can learn to integrate indigenous wisdom into contemporary environmental management approaches.

The Contributions of Traditional Ecological Knowledge

Traditional Ecological Knowledge encompasses a rich tapestry of wisdom, practices, and beliefs that contribute significantly to the preservation of ecosystems and the well-being of indigenous communities. Let's explore some notable contributions of TEK:

1. **Biodiversity conservation:** Indigenous communities have a profound understanding of local flora and fauna, often categorized by complex taxonomic systems. This knowledge helps identify keystone species, medicinal plants, and culturally significant organisms. By preserving and protecting these species, indigenous communities actively contribute to biodiversity conservation.

2. **Resource management:** Through generations of observation and experience, indigenous communities have developed sustainable resource management practices. These practices often involve limiting the extraction of natural resources to sustainable levels, employing selective harvesting techniques, and implementing traditional governance systems that ensure equitable distribution and use of resources.

3. **Fire management:** Many indigenous cultures have mastered the use of fire as a land management tool. Controlled burning helps maintain ecosystem health by reducing fuel loads, promoting nutrient cycling, and rejuvenating the growth of certain plant species. Indigenous communities employ traditional burning practices to prevent catastrophic wildfires and enhance habitat diversity.

4. **Water management:** Indigenous communities possess a deep knowledge of water systems, including rivers, lakes, and underground aquifers. They understand water's sacredness and its essential role in sustaining life. Indigenous water management practices aim to ensure the protection of water sources, maintain water quality, and promote equitable access to water for both humans and wildlife.

5. **Climate change adaptation:** Indigenous communities have adapted to environmental changes for centuries. Their knowledge of climate cycles, weather patterns, and local ecological indicators enables them to anticipate and respond to climate variability. By integrating traditional adaptation strategies with scientific approaches, indigenous communities contribute to climate change resilience.

Integrating Traditional Ecological Knowledge into Modern Practices

Integrating Traditional Ecological Knowledge with scientific approaches holds great potential for sustainable environmental management. The collaboration between indigenous communities and scientists can enhance our understanding of ecosystems, develop effective conservation strategies, and ensure the well-being of both humans and nature. Here are some ways to bridge the gap between traditional and modern knowledge systems:

- **Respect and collaboration:** Building meaningful partnerships between indigenous communities and scientists requires mutual respect, trust, and recognition of the value of each knowledge system. Collaboration should be based on equitable participation, shared decision-making, and the acknowledgment of indigenous rights and cultural protocols.

- **Knowledge exchange and co-learning:** Engaging in knowledge exchange allows indigenous communities and scientists to learn from each other's expertise. Co-learning initiatives, such as joint research projects or workshops, create opportunities for integrating traditional and scientific knowledge, fostering a more holistic understanding of ecosystems.

- **Policy and management integration:** Policies and management plans should incorporate Traditional Ecological Knowledge alongside scientific data. Recognizing indigenous perspectives and practices in policy development ensures the inclusion of diverse voices and enhances the effectiveness of conservation and resource management measures.

- **Education and capacity building:** Promoting the inclusion of Traditional Ecological Knowledge in formal education systems and scientific training programs can foster an appreciation for indigenous wisdom. By empowering indigenous youth to embrace and carry forward their traditional knowledge, we can ensure its preservation and future contributions to environmental sustainability.

It is crucial to recognize that Traditional Ecological Knowledge is not stagnant but evolves and adapts to changing circumstances. By embracing its timeless wisdom and combining it with scientific advancements, we can create a harmonious coexistence between humans and nature, paving the way for a more sustainable and inclusive future.

Subsection 4: Indigenous Technological Advancements

In this subsection, we will explore the remarkable technological advancements achieved by indigenous cultures around the world. These innovations not only demonstrate their ingenuity and resourcefulness but also challenge the commonly held belief that technological progress is exclusively attributed to Western civilizations. By examining indigenous technological achievements, we can gain a deeper appreciation for the diversity of human knowledge and the interconnectedness of human civilizations.

Introduction to Indigenous Technology

Indigenous technology refers to the practical knowledge and skills developed by indigenous peoples to meet their specific needs and adapt to their unique environments. It encompasses a wide range of disciplines, including agriculture, architecture, engineering, transportation, and communication. Indigenous technology is often closely intertwined with culture, spirituality, and sustainable practices, reflecting the deep connection between indigenous communities and their natural surroundings.

Agricultural Innovations

Indigenous communities have made significant contributions to agricultural practices, revolutionizing crop cultivation techniques and introducing innovations that have greatly impacted global food production. One such example is the creation of chinampas, floating agricultural islands constructed by the Aztecs in ancient Mesoamerica. These elevated, rectangular plots allowed efficient farming in swampy areas and dramatically increased crop yields. The chinampas system not only provided sustenance for the growing population but also helped regulate floods and protect wetland ecosystems.

Another remarkable indigenous agricultural innovation is the technique of terracing, developed by indigenous peoples in mountainous regions such as the Inca civilization in the Andes. Terraces are stepped agricultural fields built on slopes, transforming previously unusable terrain into fertile farming spaces. By preventing erosion and maximizing water retention, terracing facilitated the cultivation of various crops at high altitudes and played a crucial role in sustaining the Inca empire.

Architectural and Engineering Marvels

Indigenous cultures have also demonstrated exceptional skills in architectural design and engineering, creating magnificent structures that blend harmoniously with their surroundings. One prime example is the ancient city of Machu Picchu, constructed by the Inca civilization in Peru. The Inca employed sophisticated engineering techniques to build the city on a steep mountain ridge, using precisely cut stones that fit together without mortar. This architectural marvel not only showcased the Inca's mastery of stone masonry but also demonstrated their deep understanding of seismic stability, ensuring the structures' resilience against earthquakes.

In North America, indigenous peoples developed the technique of bark peeling to construct durable and sustainable dwellings known as wigwams or longhouses. By carefully removing bark from trees in large, intact sheets, indigenous communities were able to create flexible yet weather-resistant coverings for their homes. Additionally, the Iroquois Confederacy, an alliance of indigenous tribes in northeastern North America, implemented innovative architectural designs for their longhouses, incorporating multiple families under one roof and promoting communal living.

Transportation and Communication Systems

Indigenous cultures have devised ingenious methods of transportation and communication, relying on their profound knowledge of the natural environment. One such example is the extensive network of canals and waterways constructed by the ancient Maya civilization in Central America. These hydraulic systems facilitated the transportation of people and goods, connecting distant regions and enabling trade and cultural exchange. The Maya's understanding of hydraulics and water conservation played a crucial role in the development of their civilization.

In the Arctic region, indigenous Inuit communities mastered the art of building traditional kayaks. These lightweight and maneuverable watercraft were expertly constructed using animal skins stretched over a wooden frame. The kayaks allowed the Inuit to navigate icy waters, hunt for food, and explore vast stretches of the Arctic with great efficiency. The design and construction techniques of these kayaks continue to be revered as a testament to the Inuit's deep understanding of their marine environment.

Preservation and Sustainability

Indigenous technological advancements often prioritized sustainability and a harmonious relationship with the natural world. Indigenous communities developed innovative preservation techniques to ensure long-term food security and minimize waste. For instance, indigenous peoples in what is now the southwestern United States constructed storerooms known as granaries, designed to protect harvested crops from pests and the elements. These granaries often featured elevated foundations and ventilation systems, allowing air circulation while safeguarding the stored food.

Indigenous communities also practiced advanced techniques for resource management, exemplified by the sustainable fishing practices of the Pacific Northwest tribes. These tribes implement strategies such as fish weirs, complex wooden structures that direct fish into specific areas for harvesting while allowing the majority of the population to continue upstream for spawning. These ingenious devices ensured the availability of fish for sustenance while minimizing the impact on fish populations and their ecosystems.

Exploring Indigenous Technological Advancements

To further explore the indigenous technological advancements discussed in this subsection, you can engage in the following activities and discussions:

1. Research and document other examples of indigenous agricultural techniques from different regions around the world. Consider the impact of these techniques on food production, sustainability, and cultural practices.

2. Investigate the architecture and engineering of other indigenous civilizations, such as the pyramids of Egypt or the Great Zimbabwe. Compare and contrast these structures with indigenous architectural marvels discussed in this subsection.

3. Examine communication and transportation systems developed by indigenous cultures, such as the Inca road network in South America or the nomadic tribes' migratory routes. Reflect on how these systems influenced cultural exchange, trade, and social cohesion.

4. Discuss the importance of preserving and revitalizing indigenous technological knowledge in the face of modern-day challenges, including climate change and cultural erosion. Explore initiatives that aim to document and promote indigenous technologies.

By delving into indigenous technological advancements, we challenge the notion that innovation is a Western concept and recognize the immense contributions of indigenous cultures to human progress. These advancements not only provide valuable insights into the capabilities of indigenous peoples but also offer valuable lessons on sustainability, harmonious coexistence with nature, and the preservation of cultural heritage.

Subsection 5: Contributions to Astronomy and Mathematics

In this subsection, we will explore the significant contributions made by indigenous peoples to the fields of astronomy and mathematics. Indigenous cultures all around the world have developed extensive knowledge and understanding of celestial bodies and mathematical concepts, often using unique and innovative approaches. These contributions have played a crucial role in shaping our understanding of the universe and advancing the field of mathematics.

Indigenous Astronomy

Indigenous astronomy refers to the knowledge and practices developed by various indigenous cultures to observe and interpret celestial phenomena. Indigenous peoples have been observing the night sky for thousands of years and have developed intricate systems to understand and navigate the cosmos.

One example of indigenous astronomical knowledge is the astronomy of the Indigenous peoples of the Americas, who developed complex calendars based on celestial observations. The Mayan civilization, for instance, had a sophisticated understanding of celestial movements and created a calendar system that accurately predicted celestial events such as eclipses. They also had detailed knowledge of the cyclical movements of Venus, which they incorporated into their religious and agricultural practices.

In Australia, Aboriginal and Torres Strait Islander peoples have developed rich astronomical traditions that form an integral part of their cultural identity. They have used the positions of stars, planets, and constellations to navigate the land, track seasonal changes, and determine the availability of food sources. The Aboriginal people of the Birriliburu region, for example, have used their knowledge of the Pleiades cluster to determine the optimal timing for collecting eucalyptus gum, an important food source.

Indigenous Mathematics

Indigenous cultures have also made significant contributions to the field of mathematics, developing sophisticated mathematical systems that differ from the Eurocentric approach. Indigenous mathematics often emphasizes practical applications and problem-solving related to their cultural contexts.

One notable example is the mathematics of the Inca civilization in South America. The Inca people developed a base-10 numerical system and used a system of quipus, knotted strings, for record-keeping and mathematical calculations. The quipus served as a form of binary system, with different knots representing different numerical values. This system allowed the Inca to perform complex mathematical operations and keep extensive records of their agricultural production and census data.

Another example is the mathematics of the Yoruba people in West Africa. The Yoruba have a rich system of geometric and algebraic knowledge, which they express through their traditional art and architecture. Their understanding of symmetry, proportion, and geometric patterns has been applied to various aspects of their cultural expression, from textile design to the construction of sacred spaces.

It is important to recognize and value the contributions of indigenous peoples to astronomy and mathematics. Their unique perspectives and approaches offer valuable insights into the understanding of the universe and the development of mathematical knowledge. By incorporating indigenous knowledge into the mainstream curriculum, we can foster a more inclusive and holistic understanding of these disciplines.

Challenges and Preservation

Unfortunately, much of the indigenous knowledge of astronomy and mathematics has been marginalized or lost due to colonialism, displacement, and cultural assimilation. As a result, efforts are being made to preserve and revitalize these traditional systems of knowledge.

Indigenous communities, educators, and researchers are working together to document and transmit indigenous astronomical and mathematical knowledge to future generations. This includes initiatives to record oral traditions, study ancient texts and artifacts, and engage in collaborative research with indigenous communities.

Preserving indigenous knowledge is not only important for cultural preservation but also for expanding the scope and diversity of human knowledge. The inclusion of indigenous perspectives in astronomy and mathematics can lead to new discoveries and fresh insights that benefit all of humanity.

Exercise: Exploring Indigenous Astronomical Knowledge

To better understand the contributions of indigenous peoples to astronomy, try the following exercise:

Choose an indigenous culture that has a rich astronomical tradition, such as the Mayans, Aboriginal Australians, or the Navajo. Research their astronomical practices, including their observations of celestial bodies, their creation stories related to the cosmos, and the practical applications of their astronomical knowledge.

Write a short essay summarizing your findings and reflecting on the significance of indigenous astronomical contributions. Discuss how their understanding of the universe differs from the Eurocentric perspective and how their contributions have been overlooked or undervalued in mainstream academic discourse.

By engaging with indigenous astronomical knowledge, we can appreciate the diversity of human perspectives and broaden our understanding of the cosmos.

Section 2: Indigenous Art, Music, and Culture

Subsection 1: Indigenous Visual Arts and Crafts

Indigenous visual arts and crafts offer a profound glimpse into the rich cultural heritage of various indigenous communities around the world. The artistic expressions of indigenous peoples are deeply rooted in their traditions, spirituality, and the historical experiences they have endured. Through their creative works, indigenous artists communicate their stories, beliefs, and connections to the natural environment.

Traditional Artistic Practices

Indigenous visual arts encompass a wide range of mediums such as painting, sculpture, pottery, weaving, basketry, beadwork, and carving. These art forms have been passed down through generations, preserving cultural traditions and serving as a means of self-expression and identity.

Painting and Drawing: Indigenous paintings often depict scenes from historical events, myths, creation stories, and the natural world. The use of vibrant colors and intricate patterns is characteristic of many indigenous art styles. Natural pigments, such as minerals and plant dyes, are still used by some communities to maintain the authenticity of their artwork.

Sculpture and Carving: Sculpture and carving have a significant place in indigenous visual arts. Many indigenous cultures create sculptures to represent spiritual beings, ancestors, or sacred animals. Stone, wood, bone, and clay are commonly used materials for sculpting. Each material holds symbolic meaning and connects the artwork to the natural elements present in the indigenous communities' environment.

Weaving and Textiles: Weaving is a prominent artistic practice among many indigenous cultures. Textiles play a vital role in expressing cultural identity and preserving traditional knowledge. Indigenous weavers employ various techniques, including backstrap weaving, loom weaving, and finger weaving, to create intricate patterns and designs. These patterns often carry cultural significance, representing symbols of natural elements, ancestral stories, or community values.

Pottery and Ceramics: Indigenous pottery and ceramics date back centuries and have been integral to indigenous communities' daily lives. Different regions have distinct pottery styles, reflecting the local environment's resources and cultural practices. Indigenous potters use traditional methods such as hand-coiling or slab construction, often embellished with decorative motifs. The ceramics serve utilitarian purposes, such as storing food and water, and also hold symbolic value in religious ceremonies and rituals.

Basketry and Beadwork: Basketry and beadwork are intricate art forms that require both technical skill and creative expression. Indigenous communities have perfected the art of basketry, utilizing local plant fibers, grasses, and tree bark to create baskets of diverse shapes and sizes. These baskets serve various purposes, such as carrying and storing items, as well as for ceremonial use. Beadwork, on the other hand, involves using tiny beads to create detailed patterns and designs on clothing, jewelry, and decorative items. Each beadwork design holds cultural significance and communicates specific messages within the community.

Cultural Significance and Preservation

Indigenous visual arts and crafts are deeply intertwined with the cultural, spiritual, and social fabric of indigenous communities. They serve as vehicles for cultural preservation and intergenerational knowledge transfer. These artistic practices embody the community's identity, history, and connection to the land, reinforcing a sense of belonging and continuity.

Furthermore, indigenous visual arts play a vital role in maintaining cultural autonomy and challenging dominant narratives. By showcasing their artistic traditions and reclaiming their cultural heritage, indigenous artists resist historical erasure, misinformation, and cultural appropriation. These artistic expressions serve as a powerful means of reclaiming agency and asserting sovereignty.

Challenges and Contemporary Issues

Despite the cultural significance of indigenous visual arts and crafts, these art forms face numerous challenges and contemporary issues.

Cultural Appropriation: Indigenous art has faced exploitation and appropriation, with non-indigenous individuals and companies reproducing and profiting from indigenous cultural symbols and designs without permission or appropriate recognition. Cultural appropriation poses a significant threat to the cultural integrity of indigenous communities and undermines their ability to control and benefit from their artistic expressions.

Socio-Economic Barriers: Indigenous artists often face socio-economic barriers that hinder their ability to practice and showcase their art. Limited access to art supplies, lack of marketing platforms, and discrimination within the art industry can all impede indigenous artists' opportunities for recognition, appreciation, and financial stability.

Preserving Traditional Knowledge: In an era of globalization and rapid cultural change, there is a growing concern about preserving traditional knowledge associated with indigenous visual arts and crafts. Efforts must be made to engage younger generations in learning these art forms, as they are vital for maintaining cultural continuity and passing down indigenous artistic practices to future generations.

Promoting Indigenous Visual Arts and Crafts

Promoting and supporting indigenous visual arts and crafts is crucial for fostering cultural diversity, safeguarding indigenous cultural heritage, and creating opportunities for economic empowerment. Several strategies can be implemented to achieve these goals:

Collaboration and Partnerships: Establishing collaborative projects and partnerships between indigenous artists, cultural institutions, and educational organizations can provide platforms for showcasing indigenous visual arts and crafts. These collaborations can facilitate knowledge exchange, create mentorship opportunities, and raise awareness about the cultural significance of indigenous art forms.

Education and Cultural Appreciation: Integrating indigenous visual arts and crafts into educational curricula helps raise awareness and appreciation among students. Teaching the historical, cultural, and artistic aspects of indigenous art can foster cross-cultural understanding and combat stereotypes and misinformation. Cultural appreciation workshops and exhibitions can also be organized to invite broader community engagement.

Ethical Consumption: Supporting indigenous artists and craftspeople directly by purchasing their artwork ensures that they are benefiting from their artistic skills and tradition. Consumers should prioritize purchasing art from reputable sources that provide fair compensation and recognize the cultural and intellectual property rights of indigenous artists.

Policy and Legislation: Governments and cultural organizations should develop policies and legislation to protect indigenous intellectual property rights and prevent cultural appropriation. These policies should promote the equitable representation of indigenous visual arts and crafts in public spaces, museums, and art galleries.

Example: Traditional Navajo Weaving

One example of indigenous visual arts and crafts is traditional Navajo weaving. The Navajo people, also known as Diné, have a long-standing tradition of creating intricate textiles using a horizontal loom. Navajo weaving is highly esteemed for its technical skill, unique designs, and cultural significance.

Traditional Navajo weavers use a variety of natural materials, including hand-spun wool, and employ complex techniques to create geometric patterns and symbols infused with symbolic meaning. These designs often reflect stories from Navajo mythology and the physical and spiritual landscape of the southwestern United States.

Navajo weaving has not only served as a means of artistic expression but also played a significant role in the economic sustainability of the Navajo Nation. The beauty and craftsmanship of Navajo textiles have attracted collectors and art enthusiasts worldwide, creating economic opportunities for Navajo weavers and their communities.

However, Navajo weaving has faced challenges, including the mass-produced imitation of Navajo designs and the misappropriation of sacred symbols. Initiatives such as the Authenticity Coalition have been introduced to protect the integrity of Navajo weaving and educate consumers about the importance of purchasing authentic Navajo textiles.

In conclusion, indigenous visual arts and crafts hold immense cultural, historical, and artistic value. They are vehicles for preserving indigenous traditions, expressing identity, and challenging dominant narratives. The appreciation and support of indigenous art forms are essential for cultural diversity, intergenerational knowledge transmission, and the empowerment of indigenous communities.

Subsection 2: Influence on Contemporary Art Movements

Artistic movements throughout history have been shaped by various factors, including cultural, social, and political influences. Minority communities have played a significant role in shaping contemporary art movements, challenging traditional art practices, and bringing forth new perspectives. In this subsection, we will explore the influence of minority communities on contemporary art movements and their significant contributions to the art world.

Contemporary Art Movements and Diversity

Contemporary art movements are characterized by their commitment to experimentation, innovation, and pushing the boundaries of traditional art forms. They often emerged as responses to societal changes, challenging established norms, and reflecting the diversity of human experiences. Minority communities have actively contributed to these movements, introducing alternative narratives, engaging with their unique cultural heritage, and addressing the issues faced by marginalized populations.

The Harlem Renaissance and African American Art

One of the most prominent examples of a minority community's influence on contemporary art movements is the Harlem Renaissance in the early 20th century. The Harlem Renaissance was an intellectual and cultural movement that celebrated African American art, literature, music, and theater. It provided a platform for African American artists to showcase their talents and challenge racial stereotypes prevalent at the time.

Artists such as Aaron Douglas, Romare Bearden, and Jacob Lawrence emerged during this period, incorporating African aesthetics and themes of racial identity and pride into their artworks. Their works depicted the struggles, resilience, and achievements of African Americans, contributing to a broader recognition and appreciation of African American art and culture.

Feminist Art and Gender Representation

Another significant influence on contemporary art movements is feminism and its impact on challenging gender norms and stereotypes. Feminist art has been crucial in redefining the representation of women in art and addressing issues of gender inequality, discrimination, and objectification.

Artists like Judy Chicago, Cindy Sherman, and Kara Walker have played essential roles in feminist art movements. They have explored diverse mediums, including performance art, photography, and installations, to communicate feminist ideologies and critique established art institutions. Their works have shed light on women's experiences, advocated for reproductive rights, and celebrated the woman's body in all its forms.

Queer Art and LGBTQ+ Representation

The LGBTQ+ community has also made significant contributions to contemporary art movements, challenging conventional notions of gender and sexuality. LGBTQ+ artists have used art as a platform to express their identities, advocate for equal rights, and challenge societal prejudices.

Artists like Keith Haring, Felix Gonzalez-Torres, and Catherine Opie have used their artworks to address the HIV/AIDS crisis, explore queer identities, and challenge heteronormativity. Their art has created a visible presence for LGBTQ+

experiences within the art world, making space for dialogue, acceptance, and celebration of queer culture.

Asian American Art and Cultural Identity

Asian American artists have had a profound impact on contemporary art movements, bringing forth their unique experiences as individuals of Asian descent living in America. They explore themes of cultural identity, diaspora, immigration, and the complexities of navigating multiple cultural contexts.

Artists like Maya Lin, Nam June Paik, and Yayoi Kusama have pushed the boundaries of traditional art forms and incorporated elements of their Asian heritage into their artworks. Their contributions have not only enriched contemporary art movements but have also raised important questions about cultural assimilation, cultural preservation, and globalization.

Indigenous Art and Environmental Activism

Indigenous artists have long been at the forefront of contemporary art movements, using their art to express their connection to the land, address environmental issues, and challenge colonial narratives. Their artistic practices often incorporate traditional techniques, materials, and symbolism while engaging with contemporary themes and issues.

Artists such as Rebecca Belmore, Jaune Quick-to-See Smith, and Norval Morrisseau have used their artworks to advocate for indigenous rights, environmental conservation, and cultural revitalization. Their art serves as a powerful tool for storytelling, healing, and reclaiming indigenous culture and knowledge.

Exhibition Spaces and Representation

In addition to individual artists' contributions, the establishment of dedicated exhibition spaces and curatorial initiatives has been crucial in promoting minority artists and their works. Museums, galleries, and art institutions have played a vital role in showcasing and amplifying the voices of diverse artists, challenging the traditional canon of art history, and fostering greater inclusivity in the art world.

Initiatives such as the Studio Museum in Harlem, the Asian Art Museum, and the National Museum of the American Indian have provided platforms for minority artists to exhibit their works and engage with broader audiences. These spaces have facilitated dialogues around race, ethnicity, gender, and sexuality, allowing for a more comprehensive understanding of contemporary art movements.

Conclusion

The influence of minority communities on contemporary art movements cannot be overstated. Their contributions have added depth, diversity, and vitality to the art world, challenging established norms, and broadening our understanding of art's potential. As we navigate an increasingly interconnected and diverse world, recognizing and appreciating the contributions of minority artists is essential for fostering inclusivity, promoting social justice, and creating a more equitable art community.

Subsection 3: Indigenous Music and Instruments

Indigenous music and instruments have played a significant role in shaping the cultural identity of diverse communities throughout history. This subsection explores the rich traditions, unique instruments, and captivating rhythms that define indigenous music. We will delve into the cultural significance of these musical expressions, their connection to indigenous spirituality and storytelling, and their influence on contemporary music.

Indigenous Musical Traditions

Music holds a sacred place in indigenous cultures, serving as a means of communication, cultural preservation, and spiritual connection. Indigenous communities around the world have developed a wide range of musical traditions, each reflecting their distinct heritage, beliefs, and environments.

The musical styles vary greatly, from the vibrant drumming and chanting of Native American tribes to the soulful melodies of Aboriginal Australian didgeridoo. The rhythmic sounds and melodic patterns are often inspired by natural elements such as animals, wind, and water. Indigenous music celebrates the interconnectedness between humans and the natural world.

Instruments of Indigenous Music

Indigenous instruments are deeply rooted in the materials and resources available in specific regions. These instruments not only produce sounds but also serve as symbols of cultural identity and ancestral knowledge. Here, we will explore some of the most influential indigenous instruments.

1. **Native American Flute** : The Native American flute is a hauntingly beautiful instrument that originated in the Southwest United States. Traditionally made

from cedar or bamboo, it produces a soothing and meditative sound. The flute's unique construction allows musicians to achieve a distinct range of melodies and tones, often evoking the spirit of nature. It is widely recognized for its contribution to contemporary world music genres.

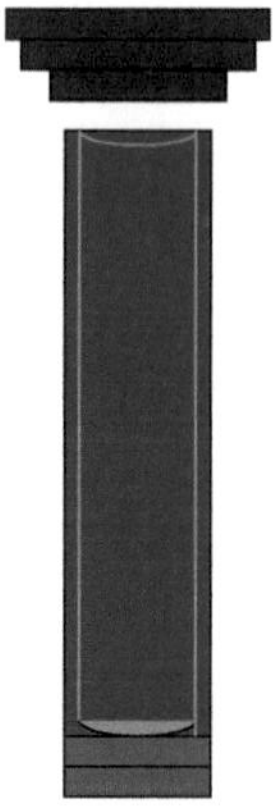

Figure 0.1: Native American Flute

2. **Australian Didgeridoo** : The didgeridoo, a wind instrument native to Australia, holds deep cultural and spiritual significance for Aboriginal communities. Traditionally made from eucalyptus branches hollowed out by termites, the didgeridoo produces a low, resonant sound. Its rhythmic patterns, created through circular breathing techniques, mimic the sounds of the natural world. Today, the didgeridoo is not only intrinsic to traditional Aboriginal music but has also gained popularity in contemporary genres.

3. **African Djembe** : The djembe, a drum originating from West Africa, embodies the vibrant rhythms and communal spirit of African music. Carved from a single piece of hardwood and covered with goatskin, the djembe produces a wide range of tones and dynamics. The drummer's hands strike the drum's surface with different techniques, creating intricate rhythms that serve as a means of communication within the community. The djembe has gained recognition worldwide and is frequently used in various music genres, including jazz, reggae, and world music.

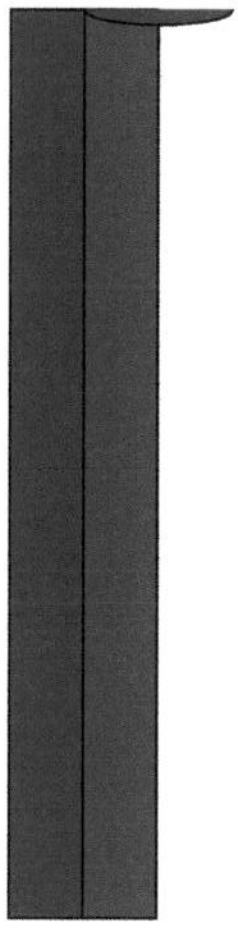

Figure 0.2: Australian Didgeridoo

Figure 0.3: African Djembe

Cultural Significance and Contemporary Influence

Indigenous music serves as a powerful tool for cultural preservation, passing down stories, histories, and values from one generation to the next. These musical traditions are deeply intertwined with indigenous spirituality and often accompany traditional rituals, ceremonies, and dances. Indigenous music represents a living connection to ancestral knowledge and serves as a means of asserting cultural identity and resilience in the face of historical marginalization.

In recent years, indigenous music has also made a significant impact on contemporary music genres. From incorporating indigenous instruments and rhythms into popular music to raising awareness about indigenous rights and environmental issues through culturally-inspired songs, indigenous musicians continue to shape the global music landscape. Their work not only bridges cultural divides but also fosters appreciation for the rich diversity of indigenous cultures.

Listening Recommendations

To truly appreciate the beauty and diversity of indigenous music, here are some recommended listening experiences:

1. "Voice of the Ancestors" by R. Carlos Nakai (Native American flute)
2. "Spirit of the Earth" by Ganga Giri (didgeridoo)
3. "Djembefola" by Mamady Keita (djembe)
4. "An Ancient Muse" by Loreena McKennitt (featuring indigenous instruments)
5. "Digging Roots" by Digging Roots (blending traditional Indigenous sounds with contemporary styles)

Immerse yourself in the captivating rhythms and unique sounds of indigenous music, and let this rich cultural heritage inspire and resonate within you.

Conclusion

Indigenous music and instruments have woven melodies and rhythms into the very fabric of human history. While often underrepresented in mainstream narratives, they carry immense cultural and spiritual significance for indigenous communities. By recognizing and appreciating the contributions of indigenous musicians, we can foster a more inclusive and diverse understanding of music's role in shaping our world. Let us embrace and celebrate the indigenous musical traditions that continue to captivate and inspire us.

Subsection 4: Cultural Traditions and Festivals

Cultural traditions and festivals play a vital role in showcasing the diversity and richness of minority contributions in history. These events provide an opportunity for communities to come together, celebrate their heritage, and preserve their cultural identity. In this section, we will explore some of the significant cultural traditions and festivals that highlight the contributions of minority groups throughout history.

Importance of Cultural Traditions and Festivals

Cultural traditions and festivals are crucial in maintaining the social fabric of communities and passing down ancestral knowledge and values to future generations. They serve as platforms for expressing cultural identity, promoting unity, and ensuring the preservation of minority cultures in a rapidly changing world.

These events often feature a variety of activities such as music, dance, storytelling, art exhibitions, food stalls, and traditional games. They create a vibrant and immersive experience for attendees, enabling them to experience the richness and uniqueness of different cultures. Additionally, cultural traditions and festivals contribute to the local economy by attracting tourists and generating revenue.

Examples of Cultural Traditions and Festivals

1. **Dia de los Muertos (Day of the Dead)**: Originating in Mexico, Day of the Dead is a traditional festival that honors and remembers deceased loved ones. It combines indigenous customs with Catholic traditions, creating a vibrant celebration filled with colorful decorations, elaborate altars (ofrendas), and lively processions. Participants gather in cemeteries, homes, and public spaces to pay homage to their ancestors through music, dance, food, and storytelling.

2. **Chinese New Year**: Celebrated by millions of people worldwide, Chinese New Year marks the beginning of the lunar calendar and is one of the most significant cultural festivals in the world. It is characterized by dragon and lion dances, traditional Chinese music, vibrant decorations (red lanterns, paper cutouts), firework displays, and a wide array of delicious food. The festival highlights Chinese cultural heritage and beliefs, emphasizing family reunion, prosperity, and good fortune for the upcoming year.

3. **Carnival**: Carnival is a vibrant and colorful festival celebrated in many countries around the world. It originated in Europe but has since spread to various regions with different cultural adaptations. The festival typically features parades, masquerade balls, music, dance performances, and elaborate costumes. It provides an opportunity for individuals to embrace their cultural diversity, express creativity, and celebrate freedom and self-expression.

4. **Holi**: Holi, also known as the Festival of Colors, is a Hindu spring festival celebrated in India and other parts of South Asia. It is characterized by the throwing of colored powders and water, symbolizing the arrival of spring and the triumph of

good over evil. Holi brings people from diverse backgrounds together, transcending social boundaries, and promoting unity and harmony.

5. **Hanami:** Hanami, meaning "flower viewing," is a traditional Japanese custom that celebrates the beauty of cherry blossoms (sakura). During this festival, people gather in parks, gardens, and temples to enjoy the transient beauty of the cherry blossoms. It involves picnicking under the blossoming trees, participating in traditional performances, and engaging in cultural activities such as tea ceremonies. Hanami is a significant cultural tradition that embodies the appreciation of nature's fleeting beauty.

Preserving and Promoting Cultural Traditions

Preserving and promoting cultural traditions and festivals is crucial for maintaining minority contributions in history. Here are some strategies that can be employed to ensure their continuity:

1. **Education and Awareness:** Schools and community organizations should incorporate the teaching of cultural traditions and festivals into their curriculum. This can help raise awareness among younger generations and instill pride in their heritage.

2. **Community Involvement:** Engaging local communities in the planning and organization of cultural events fosters a sense of ownership and encourages active participation. Collaboration between community leaders, artists, and event organizers can lead to the development of sustainable cultural traditions.

3. **Documentation and Research:** Documenting cultural traditions and festivals through photography, videos, and written records helps in their preservation. This documentation can serve as valuable resources for future generations and researchers interested in studying minority contributions.

4. **Government Support:** Governments can play a crucial role in supporting cultural traditions and festivals by providing funding, infrastructure, and policy frameworks that foster their growth and sustainability. This includes the protection of cultural heritage sites and the promotion of cultural tourism.

5. **Intercultural Exchange Programs:** Facilitating intercultural exchange programs between different communities and fostering collaborations can promote cultural understanding, appreciation, and dialogue. Such programs create opportunities for people to learn from each other, celebrate diversity, and forge meaningful connections.

In conclusion, cultural traditions and festivals are essential for recognizing and celebrating the contributions of minority groups throughout history. These events provide a platform for expressing cultural identity, promoting unity, and ensuring the preservation of minority cultures. By actively preserving and promoting these traditions, we can foster a more inclusive and diverse appreciation of history.

Chapter 2: Women's Influence Throughout History

Section 1: The Forgotten Women in Ancient Civilizations

Subsection 1: Queens and Rulers

Throughout history, there have been numerous queens and rulers who have significantly impacted their societies and left a lasting legacy. Their leadership, political skills, and influence have challenged traditional gender roles and shattered societal expectations. In this section, we will explore some remarkable queens and rulers from different cultures and time periods, highlighting their contributions and the challenges they faced.

Hatshepsut: The Female Pharaoh of Ancient Egypt

One of the most well-known female rulers in ancient history is Hatshepsut, who reigned as the fifth pharaoh of the 18th dynasty of Egypt, around 1478-1458 BCE. Despite the prevailing traditions and expectations of male rulers, Hatshepsut successfully established herself as a powerful and respected pharaoh. She is often recognized for her remarkable achievements in trade, architecture, and diplomacy.

Hatshepsut's reign was characterized by a flourishing economy and expansive trade networks. She initiated successful trading expeditions to the ancient lands of Punt, bringing back exotic goods such as myrrh, frankincense, and fragrant woods. These expeditions not only increased Egypt's wealth but also strengthened diplomatic ties with foreign nations.

In terms of architecture, Hatshepsut left a lasting legacy with her construction projects, most notably her mortuary temple at Deir el-Bahri. This impressive structure was built into the cliffs of the Theban necropolis and stood as a testament to her power and grandeur. The temple's design showcased innovative architectural techniques and showcased the splendor of the New Kingdom.

Despite her impressive achievements, after Hatshepsut's death, many of her statues and monuments were destroyed or defaced. It is believed that this was an attempt to erase her from history due to societal resistance to a female ruler. However, recent efforts in archaeological research and restoration have helped in uncovering the true extent of her influence and reign.

Catherine the Great: Enlightened Absolutism in Russia

Catherine the Great, also known as Catherine II, was Empress of Russia from 1762 until her death in 1796. She is remembered as one of the most powerful and influential rulers in Russian history. Catherine the Great played a crucial role in expanding and modernizing Russia, implementing progressive reforms, and fostering intellectual and cultural growth.

Under Catherine's rule, Russia experienced significant territorial expansion. She successfully acquired new territories, particularly in Eastern Europe, expanding the Russian Empire's borders. This expansion further solidified Russia's status as a major European power.

Catherine was a proponent of enlightenment philosophy and implemented several reforms aimed at modernizing the Russian state. She introduced legislative reforms that aimed to address social issues, improve education, and promote religious tolerance. Catherine's policies allowed for the emergence of a more educated and skilled population, contributing to the cultural and intellectual development of Russia.

Furthermore, Catherine actively supported the arts and sciences, establishing the Hermitage Museum and the Academy of Fine Arts in St. Petersburg. Her patronage of the arts brought European cultural influences to Russia, leading to a vibrant artistic and intellectual scene.

Despite her many accomplishments, Catherine also faced criticism and opposition. Some questioned her commitment to Enlightenment ideals, while others criticized her autocratic rule. Nevertheless, Catherine's reign marked a period of immense growth and transformation for Russia, and her contributions continue to shape the nation's history.

Queen Elizabeth I: The Golden Age of England

Queen Elizabeth I, also known as the "Virgin Queen," reigned over England from 1558 until her death in 1603. Her reign is often referred to as the "Golden Age" of England, characterized by stability, prosperity, and cultural achievements.

Elizabeth's astute political leadership and shrewd decision-making played a vital role in consolidating power and maintaining stability. Despite the challenges of religious conflict, she successfully brought religious unity to England by adopting a moderate religious policy that allowed for greater tolerance. This policy fostered a sense of cohesion and minimized internal conflicts.

Under Elizabeth's reign, England experienced a period of economic growth and exploration. The Elizabethan era witnessed the expansion of overseas trade, colonization efforts, and the defeat of the Spanish Armada. These accomplishments not only increased England's wealth but also strengthened its international standing.

Additionally, Elizabeth's support of the arts and literature led to a flourishing cultural scene. Many renowned playwrights, including William Shakespeare, rose to prominence during this period. The Elizabethan theater became a cultural powerhouse, producing some of the most enduring works in English literature.

Elizabeth's reign was not without challenges, particularly as a female ruler in a patriarchal society. She faced numerous political and personal threats, but her skillful diplomacy, intelligence, and resilience enabled her to navigate these hurdles successfully.

In conclusion, queens and rulers like Hatshepsut, Catherine the Great, and Queen Elizabeth I defied societal expectations and left significant impacts on their societies. Their achievements in trade, architecture, legislation, arts, and diplomacy challenged traditional gender roles and advanced their respective civilizations. Their stories serve as powerful reminders of the important contributions of women throughout history, inspiring future generations to break barriers and make their mark on the world.

Subsection 2: Warrior Women in History

Warrior women throughout history have played a significant role in shaping societies, challenging gender norms, and defending their communities. Their stories often go untold or are overshadowed by the narratives of male warriors, but their contributions are equally deserving of recognition. In this section, we will explore the presence and impact of warrior women in various civilizations and cultures.

The Rise of Warrior Women

The existence of warrior women can be traced back to ancient times when societies relied on physical strength and military prowess for survival. Despite societal expectations of women as passive and nurturing, some women defied these norms and took up arms to protect their communities.

One notable example of warrior women dates back to the time of the ancient Scythians, a nomadic people who inhabited the Eurasian Steppe. The Scythian women, known as Amazons, were skilled horse riders and archers. They played a crucial role in defending their territories and often engaged in battle alongside their male counterparts.

In Chinese history, the story of Hua Mulan stands out as an emblem of female heroism. Mulan disguised herself as a man and joined the army in place of her elderly father. Through her courage and exceptional martial arts skills, Mulan not only fought valiantly but also earned the respect of her fellow soldiers.

Examples of Warrior Women

1. Joan of Arc: One of the most well-known examples of a warrior woman is Joan of Arc. A young peasant girl from France, Joan claimed to have received divine visions instructing her to support the rightful King Charles VII and drive out the English during the Hundred Years' War. Despite facing skepticism and resistance from male military leaders, Joan led French troops to several important victories. She was eventually captured and executed for heresy, but her legacy as a symbol of female strength and bravery lives on.

2. Tomoe Gozen: In feudal Japan, Tomoe Gozen was a prominent female warrior. She served as a samurai during the Genpei War in the late 12th century and fought alongside her husband Minamoto no Yoshinaka. Tomoe was known for her exceptional skill in archery and swordsmanship, and her valor on the battlefield became legendary.

3. Dahomey Amazons: The Dahomey Amazons were a group of elite all-female warriors who served in the Kingdom of Dahomey, which is present-day Benin. These warriors were trained in combat and played a crucial role in protecting the kingdom from external threats. They were highly skilled in various weapons and known for their disciplined and fearless nature.

Challenges and Triumphs

Warrior women faced numerous challenges in their quest for equality and recognition. In many societies, their involvement in combat was viewed as a violation of traditional gender roles and subjected to societal backlash. Additionally, the historical documentation of warrior women is often fragmented or biased, leading to limited information available about their experiences.

However, despite these challenges, warrior women have made significant contributions and achieved remarkable triumphs. They have shattered stereotypes, challenged oppressive systems, and paved the way for future generations of women to pursue their dreams and aspirations.

Contemporary Significance

The stories of warrior women in history continue to inspire and empower women in the modern world. They serve as a reminder that women are not confined to traditional gender roles and have the potential to excel in any field, including military and combat.

Contemporary female soldiers, such as those serving in the armed forces of various nations, are living embodiments of the legacy of warrior women. They demonstrate that women possess the strength, courage, and resilience required to serve and protect their countries.

Moreover, the recognition of warrior women in history encourages society to reevaluate its understanding of gender roles and challenge existing stereotypes. By highlighting their contributions, we can promote inclusivity, gender equality, and cultivate a more accurate representation of history.

Discussion Questions

1. Why do you think the stories of warrior women are often overlooked or downplayed in historical narratives? 2. How do the experiences of warrior women in ancient civilizations compare to those of women in modern armed forces? 3. Can you think of any other examples of warrior women from different cultures and time periods? 4. In your opinion, why is it important to acknowledge the contributions of warrior women in history?

Further Reading

- "Warrior Women: An Archaeologist's Search for History's Hidden Heroines" by Jeannine Davis-Kimball - "Mulan's Legend and Legacy in China and the United States" edited by Lan Dong - "Joan of Arc: A History" by Helen Castor - "The Dahomey Amazons: The Remarkable True Story of the Women Who Fought in the Kingdom of Dahomey" by Robin Strand

Subsection 3: Scholars and Intellectuals

In the vast terrain of history, the contributions of women scholars and intellectuals have often been overlooked or buried beneath male-dominated narratives. However, the truth is that women have played pivotal roles in shaping the intellectual landscape throughout history. From ancient civilizations to modern societies, their intellectual prowess has been instrumental in shaping our understanding of the world.

The Suppressed Voices

For centuries, women have been systematically excluded from the halls of academia and denied access to education. Their contributions were belittled or dismissed, and their voices silenced. Nevertheless, many remarkable women defied these constraints and made significant intellectual advancements in various fields.

One such example is Hypatia of Alexandria, a renowned mathematician, philosopher, and astronomer in the 4th century AD. Despite living in an era dominated by male scholars, Hypatia's intellectual brilliance shone through. She made important contributions to mathematics, particularly in the field of Algebra and the development of astronomical instruments.

Overcoming Barriers

Despite the hurdles faced by women scholars, some managed to break barriers and leave an indelible mark on the intellectual landscape. In the 18th century, Mary Wollstonecraft emerged as a prominent voice advocating for women's rights and education. Her groundbreaking work, "A Vindication of the Rights of Woman," challenged societal norms and argued for equal educational opportunities for women.

Another notable figure, Marie Curie, revolutionized the field of science in the early 20th century. As the first woman to win a Nobel Prize, Curie's work in physics and chemistry paved the way for advancements in radioactivity research and laid the foundation for modern scientific exploration.

Contributions to Literature and Philosophy

Women scholars have made significant contributions to the world of literature and philosophy, enriching our understanding of human existence and societal dynamics. Jane Austen, an English novelist of the 19th century, explored themes of social class, morality, and romance in her iconic works such as "Pride and Prejudice" and "Sense and Sensibility." Her insightful critique of societal norms continues to resonate with readers to this day.

Simone de Beauvoir, a French philosopher, novelist, and existentialist thinker, challenged traditional notions of gender and feminism in her seminal work, "The Second Sex." Her exploration of the social and cultural construction of gender became a cornerstone in feminist philosophy, sparking critical conversations around the world.

Challenges Faced and Triumphs Achieved

Women scholars have faced numerous challenges throughout history, including prejudice, discrimination, and limited access to resources. Despite these obstacles, they have broken through barriers and left lasting legacies.

One such triumphant figure is Wangari Maathai, a Kenyan environmentalist, and political activist. Maathai founded the Green Belt Movement, which focused on environmental conservation and women's rights. Her efforts to empower women in rural communities and restore ecological balance earned her the prestigious Nobel Peace Prize in 2004.

Examples of Contemporary Women Scholars

In the modern era, women scholars continue to make groundbreaking contributions across various disciplines. Angela Davis, an American political activist and scholar, has been at the forefront of critical theory, feminism, and racial justice. Her work on prison abolition and intersectionality has influenced generations of activists and intellectuals.

Another influential figure is Chimamanda Ngozi Adichie, a Nigerian author whose works, such as "Half of a Yellow Sun" and "Americanah," tackle issues of race, identity, and feminism. Adichie's powerful storytelling has elevated the voices of African women and shed light on the complexities of the African experience.

Unlocking the Potential

To ensure a more inclusive and equitable intellectual landscape, it is essential to recognize and amplify the contributions of women scholars and intellectuals. Educational institutions must strive to provide equal opportunities and support for women pursuing academic careers.

Moreover, it is crucial for society as a whole to challenge prevailing gender biases and stereotypes that restrict the recognition and appreciation of women's intellect. By embracing the diverse range of perspectives that women bring to the table, we can unlock a wealth of untapped potential and advance knowledge in unprecedented ways.

Exploring Further

To delve deeper into the world of women scholars and intellectuals, the following resources are highly recommended:

- "A Room of One's Own" by Virginia Woolf – A seminal feminist text that explores the challenges faced by women in academia.
- "Women Who Read Are Dangerous" by Stefan Bollmann – A visual exploration of women's engagement with literature throughout history.
- "The Heretics: Adventures with the Enemies of Science" by Will Storr – A thought-provoking examination of women who challenged established scientific norms.
- "Revolting Prostitutes: The Fight for Sex Workers' Rights" by Juno Mac and Molly Smith – Explores the intersection of gender, work, and sexuality through the lens of sex workers' rights.

By engaging with these diverse perspectives, readers can develop a more comprehensive understanding of the valuable contributions made by women scholars and intellectuals throughout history.

Subsection 4: Artists and Writers

Art and literature have always played a significant role in shaping societies and reflecting the human experience. Throughout history, artists and writers from diverse backgrounds have been instrumental in challenging conventions, challenging the status quo, and broadening our understanding of the world. In this section, we will explore the contributions of artists and writers from various minority communities, highlighting their unique perspectives and the impact they have had on the cultural landscape.

The Power of Artistic Expression

Art serves as a powerful medium for self-expression, social commentary, and cultural preservation. Artists have the ability to communicate complex ideas, emotions, and stories through their work, often challenging societal norms and advocating for change. In the realm of minority contributions to art, it is crucial to acknowledge the innovative and influential voices that have emerged.

One remarkable example is the Harlem Renaissance in the early 20th century. African American artists and writers such as Langston Hughes, Zora Neale Hurston, and Jacob Lawrence were at the forefront of this artistic movement. Through their literature, poetry, and visual art, they depicted the experiences of Black Americans, celebrated their heritage, and highlighted social and racial injustice. Their works not only contributed to American literature and art but also challenged prevailing stereotypes and fostered a sense of pride and identity within the African American community.

Literature as a Mirror of Society

Literature offers a rich tapestry of human experiences, perspectives, and cultural traditions. Minority writers have used their craft to amplify marginalized voices, shed light on societal issues, and contribute to the broader literary canon. Their works provide invaluable insights into the human condition and challenge dominant narratives.

One notable example is the groundbreaking novel "Beloved" by Toni Morrison, an African American writer. This compelling and haunting story confronts the legacy of slavery and explores the lasting psychological and emotional effects on Black Americans. Morrison's lyrical prose and her ability to delve into the complexities of African American history and identity earned her numerous accolades, including the Nobel Prize in Literature.

Another significant contribution comes from the Latinx community with the works of Sandra Cisneros. Her novel "The House on Mango Street" beautifully captures the experiences of a young Mexican American girl growing up in Chicago. Through poetic language and deeply resonant storytelling, Cisneros explores themes of cultural identity, gender, and the pursuit of dreams. Her work has become a seminal text in both Latinx and American literature.

Exploring Identity and Representation

Art and literature have the power to shape cultural identity and challenge stereotypes. Minority artists and writers have used their talent to redefine representations of their communities, promoting inclusivity and fostering a more nuanced understanding of diverse cultures.

Kehinde Wiley, an African American painter, has been at the forefront of reimagining representation in art. His large-scale portraits depict black figures in the style of classical European portraiture, challenging the historical underrepresentation of Black individuals in traditional art. By placing African Americans in positions of power and dignity, Wiley challenges Eurocentric ideals and celebrates the beauty and resilience of Black culture.

In the realm of literature, Amy Tan, a Chinese American writer, has made significant contributions to the representation of Asian American experiences. Her novel "The Joy Luck Club" weaves together intergenerational stories of Chinese immigrant women and their American-born daughters. Tan delves into themes of heritage, cultural assimilation, and the complexities of mother-daughter relationships, offering a nuanced portrayal of Asian American identity.

Addressing Challenges and Evoking Change

Art and literature also serve as powerful catalysts for social change. Minority artists and writers have used their craft to address pressing societal issues, provoke thought, and foster empathy among audiences.

Renowned Nigerian writer Chinua Achebe's novel "Things Fall Apart" tackles the impact of colonization on African culture. Achebe presents a nuanced and multifaceted portrayal of Nigerian society pre and post-colonization, highlighting the devastating effects of colonialism while also celebrating the resilience of African communities. His work has been instrumental in challenging Western narratives and shaping the discourse surrounding African literature and postcolonial studies.

In the realm of art, the Guerilla Girls, a group of anonymous feminist artists, have been advocating for gender equality and raising awareness about the underrepresentation of women in the art world. Through their iconic posters and public performances, they expose gender and racial biases in the art industry, demanding greater diversity and inclusion.

The Value of Minority Contributions

The contributions of minority artists and writers are invaluable in enriching our understanding of history, challenging societal norms, and fostering a more inclusive and empathetic society. By recognizing and celebrating their work, we ensure that diverse perspectives are represented and that the cultural heritage of minority communities is preserved.

It is essential for educational institutions and curricula to provide a platform for the exploration of minority contributions in art and literature. By doing so, we amplify marginalized voices, challenge existing power structures, and pave the way for a more equitable and culturally diverse society.

Further Reading and Exploration

To delve deeper into the contributions of minority artists and writers, here are some recommended resources:

- "The Norton Anthology of African American Literature" edited by Henry Louis Gates Jr. and Valerie Smith
- "Writing America: Literary Landmarks from Walden Pond to Wounded Knee" by Shelley Fisher Fishkin
- "Art as Social Action: An Introduction to the Principles and Practices of Teaching Social Practice Art" by Gregory Sholette and Chloë Bass
- "Decolonizing Methodologies: Research and Indigenous Peoples" by Linda Tuhiwai Smith

Additionally, exploring local galleries, museums, and reading contemporary literature from diverse backgrounds can provide a broader perspective on the contributions of minority artists and writers.

Exercise: Reflect on an artwork or piece of literature that has had a profound impact on your understanding of a particular minority culture or social issue. Consider how art and literature can be transformative tools for fostering empathy and understanding.

Subsection 5: Contributions in Science and Medicine

Science and medicine have greatly benefited from the contributions of women throughout history. Despite facing significant challenges and discrimination, women have made significant advancements in various scientific disciplines and medical fields. In this section, we will explore the remarkable achievements of women scientists and their invaluable contributions to science and medicine.

Women in Scientific Research

Throughout history, women have played a crucial role in advancing scientific knowledge across various fields. Despite facing numerous obstacles, women have made groundbreaking discoveries and groundbreaking contributions to scientific research.

One notable example is Marie Curie, a Polish-born scientist who is celebrated for her pioneering research on radioactivity. Curie became the first woman to win a Nobel Prize in Physics in 1903, jointly awarded with her husband Pierre Curie and another scientist, Henri Becquerel. In 1911, she received her second Nobel Prize, this time in Chemistry, making her the first person to ever win two Nobel Prizes. Curie's research on radioactivity opened up new avenues of scientific inquiry and laid the foundation for the development of nuclear physics and medical imaging techniques.

Another influential woman in scientific research is Rosalind Franklin, a British chemist and crystallographer. Franklin's X-ray diffraction images of DNA were instrumental in the discovery of its structure. Despite her significant contributions, Franklin's work was not fully recognized during her lifetime. It was only after her death that her crucial role in the discovery of the double helix structure of DNA was acknowledged.

In recent times, women like Dr. Jennifer Doudna and Dr. Emmanuelle Charpentier have made groundbreaking discoveries in the field of gene editing. Their pioneering work on CRISPR-Cas9, a revolutionary gene editing technology, has the potential to revolutionize medicine and has opened up new possibilities for treating genetic diseases.

Women in Medicine

Women have also made significant contributions to the field of medicine throughout history. From pioneering surgical techniques to advancements in medical research, women have played a vital role in improving healthcare outcomes for individuals around the world.

One prominent figure in the history of medicine is Dr. Elizabeth Blackwell, the first woman to earn a medical degree in the United States. Blackwell's groundbreaking achievement paved the way for future generations of women to pursue careers in medicine. She went on to establish the New York Infirmary for Women and Children, a hospital staffed by women, at a time when women were largely excluded from the medical profession.

Dr. Virginia Apgar, an American obstetrical anesthesiologist, is another significant figure in the field of medicine. Apgar developed the Apgar Score, a widely-used method of assessing the health of newborn babies. Her innovation has had a profound impact on the field of neonatology and has helped in identifying and addressing potential health issues in newborns.

In recent years, Dr. Helen Brooke Taussig, a pioneering cardiologist, made significant contributions to the field of pediatric cardiology. Her groundbreaking work on the surgical treatment of children born with heart defects revolutionized the field and saved countless lives. Taussig's dedication and expertise led to the development of the "blue baby" operation, a surgical technique that corrects congenital heart defects in infants.

Challenges and Future Outlook

While women have made remarkable contributions to science and medicine, they have also faced numerous challenges and barriers along the way. Throughout history, women have been systematically excluded from educational opportunities and professional roles in scientific and medical fields. Even when they managed to overcome these barriers, their work was often disregarded or credited to male colleagues.

Today, the representation of women in science and medicine continues to be a challenge. Gender disparities persist in terms of research funding, career advancement, and leadership positions. Efforts to address these disparities and promote inclusivity in STEM fields are ongoing, with initiatives aimed at encouraging girls and young women to pursue careers in science and medicine.

In conclusion, women have made invaluable contributions to science and medicine throughout history despite facing numerous obstacles. From groundbreaking discoveries in scientific research to advancements in medical practice, women continue to shape and redefine these fields. It is crucial to recognize and celebrate their achievements to inspire future generations of women to pursue careers in science, research, and medicine.

Exercises

1. Research the life and contributions of a woman scientist or medical professional who made significant advancements in their respective fields. Write a short biography highlighting their achievements and impact.

2. Identify one area of science or medicine that is currently underrepresented by women. Discuss the potential reasons for this disparity and propose strategies to encourage more female participation in that field.

3. Explore the challenges faced by women in scientific research and medicine in different cultural and historical contexts. Compare and contrast the barriers and opportunities they encountered and the impact on their contributions.

4. Investigate the current initiatives and programs that aim to promote gender equality and inclusivity in STEM fields. Analyze their effectiveness and propose additional measures to address gender disparities.

5. Imagine you are a female scientist in a historically male-dominated field. Write a personal reflection on the challenges you would face and the strategies you would employ to overcome those barriers and succeed in your career.

Resources

- Books:
  - "Hidden Figures" by Margot Lee Shetterly
  - "Rise of the Rocket Girls: The Women Who Propelled Us, from Missiles to the Moon to Mars" by Nathalia Holt
  - "The Immortal Life of Henrietta Lacks" by Rebecca Skloot
- Websites:
  - National Women's History Museum - Women in STEM: *www.womenshistory.org/explore/topics/women-stem*
  - The Guardian - Women in Science: *www.theguardian.com/science/women-in-science*
  - The New York Times - Women in Medicine: *www.nytimes.com/topic/subject/women-in-medicine*

Key Concepts

- Women have made significant contributions to scientific research and medicine throughout history.
- Marie Curie, Rosalind Franklin, Dr. Jennifer Doudna, and Dr. Emmanuelle Charpentier are notable women who have made groundbreaking discoveries in science.
- Dr. Elizabeth Blackwell, Dr. Virginia Apgar, and Dr. Helen Brooke Taussig have made significant contributions to the field of medicine.
- Women in science and medicine have faced challenges such as gender disparities, exclusion, and lack of recognition.
- Efforts to promote inclusivity and gender equality in STEM fields are ongoing.

Section 2: Women's Roles in Social Movements

Subsection 1: Suffrage and Women's Rights Movement

The suffrage and women's rights movement is a groundbreaking historical movement that sought to secure equal rights and voting rights for women. It was a significant aspect of the broader struggle for gender equality and social justice. In this subsection, we will delve into the key events, influential figures, and the lasting impact of the suffrage and women's rights movement.

Background: Pre-Modern Women's Rights

Before examining the suffrage movement, it is essential to understand the historical context of women's rights. Throughout history, women have faced discrimination and limited opportunities in various societies. In pre-modern times, women were often relegated to domestic roles and were deprived of basic rights and privileges enjoyed by men. The concept of women's rights gained traction during the Enlightenment period, which emphasized reason, liberty, and equality.

Seneca Falls Convention: The Birth of the Suffrage Movement

One of the most pivotal moments in the history of women's rights was the Seneca Falls Convention of 1848. Held in Seneca Falls, New York, it marked the birth of the suffrage and women's rights movement in the United States. Organized by prominent suffragists Elizabeth Cady Stanton and Lucretia Mott, the convention brought together both women and men to advocate for women's rights.

At the Seneca Falls Convention, the attendees drafted a groundbreaking document known as the Declaration of Sentiments. Modeled after the Declaration of Independence, it demanded equal rights for women in various spheres of life, including the right to vote. The Declaration of Sentiments became a rallying cry for the suffrage movement and laid the foundation for future activism.

Key Figures: Suffragists and Women's Rights Activists

The suffrage and women's rights movement was propelled forward by numerous courageous and tenacious individuals who dedicated their lives to the cause. These individuals played pivotal roles in advancing women's rights and shaping the movement's trajectory.

Elizabeth Cady Stanton, an ardent suffragist, served as a leading voice in the movement. She co-organized the Seneca Falls Convention and played a crucial role in drafting the Declaration of Sentiments. Stanton's tireless advocacy and brilliant speeches resonated with audiences, and she became a driving force in the fight for women's suffrage.

Another influential figure was Susan B. Anthony, a dedicated suffragist and abolitionist. Anthony played a pivotal role in campaigning for women's voting rights and was instrumental in establishing organizations such as the National Woman Suffrage Association. Her tireless efforts laid the groundwork for future suffrage victories.

Milestones: Suffrage Victories and Achievements

The suffrage and women's rights movement witnessed several significant milestones and achievements over the years. These milestones were crucial in expanding women's rights and progressing towards gender equality.

One of the major milestones was the passage of the Nineteenth Amendment to the United States Constitution in 1920. This amendment granted women the right to vote, marking a historic victory for the suffrage movement. The tireless efforts of suffragists like Stanton and Anthony, along with countless others, finally paid off, securing a fundamental right for women.

Another remarkable achievement was the formation of the National Women's Suffrage Association (NWSA) and the American Woman Suffrage Association (AWSA). These organizations played a crucial role in coordinating activism, lobbying for suffrage legislation, and raising awareness about women's rights.

Legacy and Impact: Transforming Gender Roles and Politics

The suffrage and women's rights movement had a profound and lasting impact on society, transforming gender roles and politics. The movement challenged traditional norms and paved the way for women's increased participation in politics, education, and the workforce.

In the political arena, the suffrage movement led to increased representation for women, both as voters and elected officials. Women's voices and perspectives became integral to the decision-making process, and policies began to address gender equity. The suffrage movement also inspired subsequent waves of feminist activism, leading to further advancements in women's rights.

Beyond politics, the suffrage movement sparked broader social changes. It challenged traditional gender expectations, empowering women to pursue education and careers. The movement played a vital role in reshaping societal perceptions of women's capabilities and potential.

Contemporary Challenges: Continuing the Fight for Equality

While the suffrage movement achieved significant victories, challenges and inequalities persist to this day. Women still face barriers to equal pay, representation in leadership positions, and protection from gender-based violence. It is critical to recognize that the fight for gender equality is ongoing and requires continued activism and awareness.

Conclusion

The suffrage and women's rights movement was a pivotal moment in the history of gender equality. It brought about significant social and political changes, securing the right to vote for women and challenging traditional gender norms. The bravery and determination of suffragists and women's rights activists continue to inspire future generations in the ongoing pursuit of gender equality and social justice.

Subsection 2: Influence in Civil Rights Movements

In this subsection, we will explore the influence of women in various civil rights movements throughout history. Women have played significant roles in fighting for social justice and equality, often facing multiple layers of discrimination based on their gender, race, and socioeconomic status. Their contributions to civil rights movements have been instrumental in shaping the societies we live in today.

The Power of Women's Leadership

Women have consistently played pivotal roles in civil rights movements across different cultures and time periods. Their leadership, organizational skills, and ability to mobilize communities have been crucial in driving social change. One of the earliest examples of women's influence in civil rights movements is the suffrage movement, which fought for women's right to vote. Figures like Susan B. Anthony and Elizabeth Cady Stanton led the charge, paving the way for gender equality and political representation.

Warrior Women in the Fight for Rights

Women have not only been at the forefront of peaceful civil rights movements but have also made significant contributions as warriors and fighters. In the African American civil rights movement, women like Fannie Lou Hamer and Rosa Parks displayed immense courage and strength as they advocated for racial equality. Their acts of resistance, such as the Montgomery bus boycott and the Freedom Rides, amplified the message of the movement and inspired others to join the fight for justice.

Intellectual Prowess and Advocacy

Women have also made invaluable contributions as scholars and intellectuals in civil rights movements. Figures like Angela Davis and Audre Lorde challenged societal norms through their writings and speeches, addressing issues of race, gender, and class. Their work highlighted the intersectionality of oppression and the need for a comprehensive understanding of social justice.

Artistic Expressions of Resistance

Art has always been a powerful tool for social change, and women have harnessed its potential to challenge discrimination and advocate for civil rights. In the Civil

Rights Movement of the 1960s, artists like Nina Simone used their music to empower and unify communities. Simone's songs, such as "To Be Young, Gifted, and Black," became anthems of resilience and hope.

Influence in Contemporary Movements

Women continue to make significant contributions to civil rights movements in contemporary society. In the fight for LGBTQ+ rights, figures like Marsha P. Johnson and Sylvia Rivera were instrumental in the Stonewall Riots, which sparked a new era of activism. Their efforts laid the foundation for the modern LGBTQ+ rights movement and continue to inspire the ongoing fight for equality.

Challenges and Progress

While women have made significant strides in civil rights movements, they continue to face unique challenges and forms of discrimination. Intersectionality, a concept coined by scholar Kimberlé Crenshaw, recognizes the overlapping systems of oppression that women may face, including racism, sexism, homophobia, and economic inequality. Acknowledging and addressing these challenges is crucial for creating inclusive and effective movements.

Examining Further

To further explore the influence of women in civil rights movements, consider the following resources:

- "Sisters in the Struggle: African American Women in the Civil Rights-Black Power Movement" by Bettye Collier-Thomas and V.P. Franklin
- "Freedom Is a Constant Struggle: Ferguson, Palestine, and the Foundations of a Movement" by Angela Y. Davis
- "Suffrage: Women's Long Battle for the Vote" by Ellen Carol DuBois
- "When Everything Changed: The Amazing Journey of American Women from 1960 to the Present" by Gail Collins

Conclusion

Women have been instrumental in shaping civil rights movements throughout history. Their leadership, advocacy, and artistic expressions of resistance have challenged the status quo and propelled social change forward. Recognizing and amplifying the influence of women in civil rights movements is crucial for creating a more inclusive and equitable society.

Subsection 3: Women's Contributions to Labor Movements

In this section, we will explore the significant contributions that women have made to labor movements throughout history. Women have played crucial roles in advocating for workers' rights, fighting for fair wages, and challenging oppressive working conditions. Their activism and determination have been instrumental in shaping labor movements and ensuring better working conditions and opportunities for all.

The Struggle for Equal Pay

One of the key issues that women have consistently fought for in labor movements is equal pay. Historically, women have faced significant wage disparities compared to their male counterparts, often earning less for doing the same work. This discrimination not only undermines women's financial independence but also perpetuates gender inequality in the workplace.

To address this issue, women in labor movements have advocated for fair and equal pay, demanding that employers eliminate wage gaps based on gender. They have conducted research, organized protests, and lobbied for policy changes to promote pay equity. Thanks to their persistent efforts, progress has been made in closing the gender pay gap, although more work remains to be done.

Breaking Gender Stereotypes in Occupations

Women have also played a pivotal role in challenging gender stereotypes associated with certain occupations. Traditionally, many professions were considered "male-dominated," and women faced significant barriers to entry and advancement in these fields. However, through labor movements, women have fought for equal access to employment opportunities and dismantled discriminatory hiring practices.

For example, during the early 20th century in the United States, the International Ladies' Garment Workers' Union (ILGWU) fought for better working conditions and wages for women working in the garment industry. Their efforts not only improved the lives of female garment workers but also challenged the notion that certain occupations were exclusively for men.

Labor movements led by women have paved the way for increased representation of women in traditionally male-dominated fields such as engineering, science, and technology. By breaking gender barriers, women have expanded the possibilities for future generations, ensuring that all individuals have the opportunity to pursue their career aspirations regardless of gender.

Maternity Leave and Family-Friendly Policies

The struggle for maternity leave and family-friendly policies has long been a focus of women's contributions to labor movements. Historically, women faced immense challenges in reconciling their work and family responsibilities due to the lack of supports in the workplace. This issue disproportionately affected women, as they often shouldered the bulk of caregiving duties.

Through labor movements, women have fought for the implementation of maternity leave policies that provide job security and financial assistance to new mothers. They have advocated for inclusive family leave policies that recognize and support all caregivers, regardless of gender.

The efforts of women in labor movements have contributed to the adoption of policies such as paid family leave, flexible work arrangements, and affordable childcare options. These policies aim to create a more equitable and family-friendly work environment that values the well-being of employees and promotes work-life balance.

Addressing Workplace Harassment and Discrimination

Women in labor movements have also been at the forefront of efforts to address workplace harassment and discrimination. Historically, women have faced pervasive gender-based discrimination, including sexual harassment, unequal treatment, and limited opportunities for promotion and advancement.

Through collective action and advocacy, women in labor movements have successfully pushed for policies and legislation aimed at preventing and addressing workplace harassment and discrimination. They have raised awareness, facilitated discussions, and provided support systems for workers who have experienced harassment.

Additionally, women's contributions to labor movements have emphasized the importance of intersectionality. They have recognized that women from diverse backgrounds face unique challenges and have fought for inclusive policies and practices that address the needs of all women, including those from marginalized communities.

Case Study: The Coalition of Immokalee Workers

A notable example of women's contributions to labor movements is the Coalition of Immokalee Workers (CIW), an organization of farmworkers in Florida, United States. The CIW includes a significant number of women who have been at the forefront of campaigns seeking fair wages and improved working conditions in the agricultural industry.

Led by women, the CIW has successfully advocated for the Fair Food Program, which ensures fair wages, worker protections, and a zero-tolerance policy for sexual harassment and abuse. The organization's efforts have transformed the lives of farmworkers, empowering them to speak up against exploitation and demand fair treatment.

The case of the CIW exemplifies the essential role that women play in labor movements and their determination to challenge systemic injustices in pursuit of a more equitable society.

Conclusion

Women have made significant contributions to labor movements, fighting for equal pay, breaking gender stereotypes in occupations, advocating for family-friendly policies, addressing workplace harassment and discrimination, and championing the rights of marginalized communities. Their resilience and activism have shaped labor movements throughout history and have paved the way for greater equality and justice in the workplace.

It is through acknowledging and amplifying the contributions of women in labor movements that we can fully appreciate the collective efforts that have resulted in improved working conditions and rights for all individuals. As we move forward, it is crucial to continue supporting and amplifying women's voices in labor movements to ensure continued progress and create a more inclusive and fair society for future generations.

Subsection 4: LGBTQ+ Activism and Women

LGBTQ+ activism has played a crucial role in advocating for equal rights and challenging societal norms and prejudices. Throughout history, women have played a significant part in these movements, contributing to the progress and recognition of LGBTQ+ rights. In this subsection, we will explore the intersectionality of LGBTQ+ activism and women, highlighting the key contributions, challenges, and advancements made by women within the LGBTQ+ rights movement.

Contributions of Women in LGBTQ+ Activism

Women have made substantial contributions to LGBTQ+ activism, fighting for inclusivity, acceptance, and equal rights for all individuals, regardless of their sexual orientation or gender identity. Their efforts have led to significant gains in legal protections, social acceptance, and the advancement of LGBTQ+ rights globally.

One of the notable contributions of women in LGBTQ+ activism is their involvement in organizing and mobilizing grassroots movements. Women-led LGBTQ+ organizations, such as the National Center for Lesbian Rights and the Lesbian Avengers, have played a pivotal role in raising awareness about LGBTQ+ issues, advocating for policy changes, and providing support to the community.

Moreover, women have been at the forefront of LGBTQ+ pride marches and protests, raising their voices against discrimination and demanding equal rights. Their visibility and activism have helped challenge stereotypes, educate the broader population, and create a sense of community and belonging for LGBTQ+ individuals.

Challenges and Obstacles Faced by Women in LGBTQ+ Activism

While women have made significant contributions to LGBTQ+ activism, they have also faced unique challenges and obstacles within these movements. These challenges stem from both sexism and homophobia, as women often face marginalization and exclusion within LGBTQ+ spaces.

One prevalent challenge is the erasure of women's voices and experiences within the LGBTQ+ movement. Historically, LGBTQ+ activism has been predominantly led by cisgender gay men, and women have often been sidelined or overlooked. This erasure not only undermines the achievements and struggles of women but also perpetuates a narrow understanding of LGBTQ+ issues.

Women in LGBTQ+ activism also face intersecting discrimination based on their gender and sexual orientation. They often encounter misogyny and sexism within the broader society and even within LGBTQ+ communities. This sexism can manifest in the form of gender-based violence, lack of representation, and limited leadership opportunities.

Additionally, women who identify as lesbian or bisexual often face further marginalization due to biphobia and lesbophobia. This double discrimination makes it crucial to address specific issues faced by lesbian and bisexual women within LGBTQ+ activism, ensuring inclusivity and equal representation for all.

Advancements and Achievements

Despite the challenges, women in LGBTQ+ activism have achieved significant advancements in advancing LGBTQ+ rights and creating more inclusive societies. Some key achievements include:

- **Legal Victories:** Women have been instrumental in advocating for legal protections for LGBTQ+ individuals. They have played key roles in landmark legal battles, such as the fight for marriage equality, adoption rights, and workplace discrimination protections.
- **Transgender Rights Advocacy:** Women have been crucial allies and activists in advocating for the rights and visibility of transgender individuals. They have been at the forefront of campaigns for gender-affirming healthcare, legal recognition of gender identity, and challenging discriminatory policies.
- **Intersectional Activism:** Women in LGBTQ+ activism have emphasized the importance of intersectionality, recognizing the interconnections between race, gender, and sexual orientation. Their advocacy work highlights the specific experiences and challenges faced by LGBTQ+ women of color, amplifying their voices and fighting for their rights.
- **Impact on Mainstream Culture:** Women in LGBTQ+ activism have made significant contributions to mainstream culture, challenging heteronormative narratives and representation. Through artistic expressions, literature, and media, they have broadened the visibility of LGBTQ+ experiences and inspired societal change.

Resources and Support for Women in LGBTQ+ Activism

For women interested in getting involved in LGBTQ+ activism, numerous resources and support networks are available. These organizations provide platforms for advocacy, community-building, and empowerment:

- **Emily's List** - An organization dedicated to supporting and electing pro-choice Democratic women to office, including women advocating for LGBTQ+ rights.
- **LGBTQ+ Women's Organizations** - Organizations like the National Center for Lesbian Rights, Lesbians Who Tech, and the Equality Federation provide resources, networking opportunities, and educational programs specifically designed for LGBTQ+ women.

- **Local LGBTQ+ Community Centers** - Many LGBTQ+ community centers offer support groups, workshops, and volunteer opportunities for women interested in getting involved in LGBTQ+ activism.
- **Mentorship Programs** - Mentorship programs, such as the LGBTQ Victory Institute's Women Out to Win program, connect aspiring LGBTQ+ activists with experienced mentors who offer guidance and support.

Conclusion

Women have played a vital and transformative role in LGBTQ+ activism, advancing the rights and visibility of LGBTQ+ individuals. Their contributions, despite the challenges they face, have led to significant progress in achieving equality and acceptance. By amplifying their voices, emphasizing intersectionality, and advocating for inclusivity, women continue to shape and redefine the LGBTQ+ rights movement. It is essential to recognize and support their efforts as we strive for a more inclusive and equitable society.

Chapter 3: LGBTQ+ Contributions and Impact

Section 1: LGBTQ+ Historical Figures and Icons

Subsection 1: Writers and Poets

In this subsection, we will explore the important contributions of writers and poets from LGBTQ+ communities throughout history. Their works have not only provided artistic and literary value but have also challenged societal norms and paved the way for social change. We will delve into the impact of their writings, the challenges they faced, and the lasting legacy they have left behind.

The Power of LGBTQ+ Literature

Literature has always played a crucial role in shaping societies and challenging established norms. LGBTQ+ writers and poets have been at the forefront of using literature as a tool for self-expression, advocacy, and social critique.

One of the most influential LGBTQ+ writers of the 20th century was James Baldwin. Through his novels, essays, and plays, Baldwin explored themes of race, sexuality, and identity. His novel "Giovanni's Room" (1956) vividly depicted a homosexual relationship, breaking the silence surrounding same-sex love during a time of immense social stigma.

Another notable writer is Virginia Woolf, a pioneering figure in modernist literature. Woolf's novel "Orlando" (1928) challenges conventional notions of gender and identity, presenting a protagonist who changes gender and lives through several centuries. This novel is considered a landmark in LGBTQ+ literature for its exploration of gender fluidity and the limitations of traditional gender roles.

Challenges Faced by LGBTQ+ Writers

LGBTQ+ writers and poets have often faced immense challenges due to their sexual orientation or gender identity. Throughout history, many were forced to hide their true selves and adopt pseudonyms or write under ambiguous identities to avoid persecution and censorship.

One of the most notable examples is Oscar Wilde, a renowned playwright and poet from the late 19th century. Wilde faced public disgrace and legal consequences when his homosexuality was exposed. His trial and subsequent imprisonment had a profound impact on his life and career, as he was stigmatized and limited in his creative output.

Even after legal advancements and increased acceptance, LGBTQ+ writers and poets continue to face challenges today. They often struggle to find publishers and readers who are willing to engage with their work. Many LGBTQ+ authors are also subjected to gatekeeping and discrimination within literary circles, which can hinder their career prospects and visibility.

The Impact of LGBTQ+ Writing on Society

LGBTQ+ writing has had a profound impact on society, challenging mainstream perceptions, and fostering understanding and acceptance. These literary works have played a crucial role in both personal and collective journeys towards equality and social change.

For instance, the poetry and prose of Audre Lorde, a Black lesbian feminist writer, have been instrumental in giving voice to marginalized communities. Lorde's powerful writings explore the intersections of race, gender, and sexuality, addressing themes of racism, sexism, and homophobia. Her collection of essays in "Sister Outsider" (1984) continues to inspire and empower readers, promoting activism and self-advocacy.

Modern LGBTQ+ literature continues to push boundaries and expand representation. Authors like Ocean Vuong ("On Earth We're Briefly Gorgeous," 2019) and Carmen Maria Machado ("Her Body and Other Parties," 2017) have garnered critical acclaim for their exploration of queer experiences, bringing diverse narratives to the forefront.

Resources and Further Reading

- Baldwin, James. "Giovanni's Room." Vintage, 2013. - Woolf, Virginia. "Orlando." Penguin, 2000. - Lorde, Audre. "Sister Outsider: Essays and Speeches." Crossing Press Feminist Series, 2007. - Vuong, Ocean. "On Earth We're Briefly Gorgeous."

Penguin Press, 2019. - Machado, Carmen Maria. "Her Body and Other Parties." Graywolf Press, 2017.

Further exploration of LGBTQ+ literature can greatly enrich our understanding of the LGBTQ+ experience and contribute to a more inclusive and accepting society. By acknowledging and celebrating the immense contributions of LGBTQ+ writers and poets, we broaden our perspectives and foster a deeper appreciation for the power of literature in shaping our collective consciousness.

Subsection 2: Artists and Performers

In this subsection, we will explore the rich history of LGBTQ+ artists and performers who have made significant contributions to the arts and entertainment industry. From painters to actors, musicians to dancers, these individuals have not only shaped and influenced their respective fields but have also played an important role in promoting LGBTQ+ visibility and acceptance.

Artists

The world of art has been greatly influenced by LGBTQ+ artists who have brought their unique perspectives and experiences to their creations. They have challenged societal norms, explored themes of identity and sexuality, and offered new ways of understanding the world.

One prominent LGBTQ+ artist is Frida Kahlo, a Mexican painter known for her surreal and symbolic self-portraits. Through her art, Kahlo expressed her bisexual identity, feminine strength, and struggles with physical and emotional pain. Her works continue to inspire and resonate with audiences worldwide.

Another artist of significance is Keith Haring, an American pop artist and activist. Haring's bold and vibrant artwork often depicted themes of love, unity, and queer culture. He used his art to raise awareness about the AIDS epidemic and to advocate for LGBTQ+ rights. Haring's influence can be seen in contemporary street art and pop culture.

Performers

LGBTQ+ performers have played a vital role in shaping the entertainment industry. They have used their talent, charm, and unique perspectives to captivate audiences and break down barriers.

One iconic LGBTQ+ performer is RuPaul, a drag queen, singer, and television personality. Known for his charisma and larger-than-life personality, RuPaul has become a global phenomenon. Through his reality television show "RuPaul's Drag

Race," he has provided a platform for drag queens to showcase their artistry and has helped popularize drag as a form of entertainment.

Broadway has also seen the contributions of LGBTQ+ performers. Figures like Harvey Fierstein, an actor and playwright, have brought LGBTQ+ stories to the forefront. Fierstein's play "Torch Song Trilogy" explored themes of gay identity, love, and family, and earned him multiple Tony Awards. His work paved the way for more LGBTQ+ stories to be told on stage.

Impact and Influence

The contributions of LGBTQ+ artists and performers extend beyond their individual works. Their influence has helped shape the cultural landscape, challenging stereotypes and promoting acceptance.

By showcasing diverse love stories and creating relatable queer characters, LGBTQ+ artists and performers have helped normalize LGBTQ+ identities in mainstream media. They have paved the way for greater representation in film, television, and theater, giving LGBTQ+ individuals and communities a sense of visibility and validation.

Their art and performances have become a means of self-expression and resistance, fostering a sense of community and empowerment among LGBTQ+ individuals. LGBTQ+ artists and performers continue to push boundaries, inspiring future generations to embrace their authentic selves and pursue their creative passions.

Exercises

1. Research and analyze the works of Frida Kahlo or Keith Haring. Discuss how their art reflects their LGBTQ+ identity and the impact it has had on the art world.

2. Watch an episode of "RuPaul's Drag Race" and reflect on the significance of the show for LGBTQ+ representation. Discuss the challenges and achievements of drag queens in the entertainment industry.

3. Choose a Broadway musical or play that explores LGBTQ+ themes. Write a review of the production, highlighting its cultural significance and impact on LGBTQ+ representation in theater.

4. Research other LGBTQ+ artists and performers who have made important contributions to their respective fields. Create a visual presentation showcasing their work and the impact they have had on society.

Further Reading

1. "Frida Kahlo: Making Her Self Up" by Claire Wilcox and Circe Henestrosa 2. "Keith Haring: The Authorized Biography" by John Gruen 3. "The Diva Rules: Ditch the Drama, Find Your Strength, and Sparkle Your Way to the Top" by Michelle Visage 4. "The LGBT Artists Archive: Keith Haring" by Jonathan David Katz 5. "The Drag Queen Anthology: The Absolutely Fabulous but Flawlessly Customary World of Female Impersonators" by Steven T. Seagle

Subsection 3: LGBTQ+ Activists and Advocates

In the fight for LGBTQ+ rights and equality, activists and advocates have played a crucial role. These individuals have dedicated their lives to challenging social norms, fighting discrimination, and promoting acceptance and inclusivity. Their tireless efforts have led to significant advancements in LGBTQ+ rights, changing societal attitudes, and fostering a more inclusive world. In this section, we will explore the contributions and achievements of LGBTQ+ activists and advocates across different fields.

Harvey Milk: A Trailblazing Politician

Harvey Milk was a prominent LGBTQ+ advocate and the first openly gay elected official in the United States. In 1977, he won a seat on the San Francisco Board of Supervisors, becoming a symbol of hope and inspiration for LGBTQ+ individuals. Milk advocated for equality and fought against discrimination, particularly targeting anti-LGBTQ+ laws and policies. Tragically, Milk's life was cut short when he was assassinated in 1978, but his legacy continues to inspire LGBTQ+ activists and advocates worldwide.

Challenge and Progress: Marriage Equality One of the key milestones in the LGBTQ+ rights movement is the fight for marriage equality. LGBTQ+ activists and advocates have played a pivotal role in challenging societal norms and advocating for the recognition of same-sex marriage. The groundbreaking work of organizations such as Lambda Legal and the American Civil Liberties Union (ACLU) has led to significant advancements in this area. Landmark legal cases, such as Obergefell v. Hodges in 2015, resulted in the legalization of same-sex marriage in the United States. This achievement represents a significant step forward in the fight for LGBTQ+ rights and equality.

Intersectionality and LGBTQ+ Advocacy LGBTQ+ activism recognizes the importance of intersectionality, acknowledging that different forms of discrimination intersect and impact marginalized communities. Activists and advocates, both from within the LGBTQ+ community and allied groups, have worked to address intersectional issues and amplify the voices of those who face multiple forms of discrimination. Intersectional LGBTQ+ organizations such as the National Queer Asian Pacific Islander Alliance (NQAPIA) and Black Lives Matter have been at the forefront of this movement, advocating for the rights of LGBTQ+ individuals of diverse racial and ethnic backgrounds.

Transgender Rights: Laverne Cox and Janet Mock

Laverne Cox and Janet Mock are two influential transgender activists who have made significant contributions to the fight for transgender rights and visibility. As advocates and role models, they have raised awareness about transgender issues and challenged societal stereotypes and stigma.

Transgender Visibility and Advocacy Laverne Cox, known for her role in the hit series "Orange Is the New Black," has used her platform to advocate for transgender rights. Cox has been vocal about the importance of transgender visibility in media and has worked tirelessly to promote acceptance and understanding. By sharing her own experiences and advocating for policy changes, she has become a strong voice for the transgender community.

Elevating Transgender Voices Janet Mock, an author, television host, and transgender rights advocate, has been instrumental in elevating transgender voices and sharing their stories. Through her best-selling memoir, "Redefining Realness," and her work as a writer and producer, Mock has brought attention to the unique challenges faced by transgender individuals. Her advocacy focuses on transgender youth, intersectionality, and the importance of inclusive healthcare and legal protections.

The Fight for Transgender Rights Transgender rights continue to be a significant focus of LGBTQ+ activism. Transgender activists and advocates are working to secure legal protections against discrimination, improve access to healthcare, and promote transgender inclusivity in schools and workplaces. Organizations such as the Transgender Legal Defense & Education Fund (TLDEF) and the National Center for Transgender Equality (NCTE) are dedicated to fighting for transgender rights and improving the lives of transgender individuals.

Youth Advocacy: The Trevor Project and GLSEN

The Trevor Project and GLSEN (Gay, Lesbian, and Straight Education Network) are two prominent organizations that focus on LGBTQ+ youth advocacy. They provide support, resources, and educational initiatives to empower young people and create safer environments in schools and communities.

The Trevor Project: Saving LGBTQ+ Lives The Trevor Project is a leading organization focused on suicide prevention among LGBTQ+ youth. Through its 24/7 crisis hotline, online chat, and text support services, the Trevor Project offers immediate help to those in crisis. The organization also provides educational programs and resources to promote mental health and well-being within the LGBTQ+ community.

GLSEN: Creating Safe Schools GLSEN works to create safe and inclusive school environments for LGBTQ+ students. The organization provides training, resources, and support to educators, administrators, and students to combat bullying, harassment, and discrimination. GLSEN's initiatives, such as the Day of Silence and the GSA (Gay-Straight Alliance) network, help foster acceptance and understanding among students and promote LGBTQ+ inclusion.

Addressing Mental Health and Well-being LGBTQ+ youth face higher rates of mental health challenges, including depression and suicidal ideation. LGBTQ+ activists and advocates have been instrumental in raising awareness about these issues and advocating for accessible and inclusive mental health services. Their efforts contribute to creating a support system that addresses the unique needs of LGBTQ+ individuals and reduces the stigma surrounding mental health.

The Power of Visibility: Ellen DeGeneres and RuPaul

Ellen DeGeneres and RuPaul are well-known LGBTQ+ advocates who have used their success in the entertainment industry to increase LGBTQ+ visibility and promote acceptance.

The Ellen DeGeneres Show: Challenging Stereotypes Ellen DeGeneres, through her widely popular talk show, has become a prominent advocate for LGBTQ+ rights and visibility. By publicly coming out as gay in 1997, DeGeneres sparked conversations about LGBTQ+ issues and challenged stereotypes. Her show has provided a platform for LGBTQ+ individuals and stories, helping to educate and inspire audiences worldwide.

RuPaul's Drag Race: Embracing Authenticity RuPaul's Drag Race, a reality competition series, has not only brought drag culture into the mainstream but has also provided a platform for LGBTQ+ individuals to showcase their talents and express their authentic selves. Through his work on the show, RuPaul has championed self-acceptance, self-expression, and LGBTQ+ visibility. The show's popularity has helped break down barriers and build bridges of understanding.

The Importance of Representation LGBTQ+ representation in media and entertainment plays a vital role in shaping societal attitudes and challenging stereotypes. By showcasing diverse LGBTQ+ stories and experiences, advocates like DeGeneres and RuPaul contribute to a more inclusive narrative, paving the way for greater acceptance and understanding.

Key Takeaways

- LGBTQ+ activists and advocates have played a crucial role in the fight for LGBTQ+ rights and equality.
- Their efforts have led to significant advancements in areas such as marriage equality, transgender rights, and LGBTQ+ youth advocacy.
- Activists like Harvey Milk, Laverne Cox, and Janet Mock have challenged societal norms and advocated for greater acceptance and inclusivity.
- Organizations such as the Trevor Project and GLSEN provide support, resources, and educational initiatives to empower LGBTQ+ youth and create safer environments.
- LGBTQ+ visibility in media and entertainment, represented by individuals like Ellen DeGeneres and RuPaul, helps challenge stereotypes and promote acceptance.
- Intersectionality is a crucial aspect of LGBTQ+ advocacy, recognizing the interconnectedness of multiple forms of discrimination.

By recognizing the contributions of LGBTQ+ activists and advocates, we gain a deeper understanding of the challenges they have faced and the progress they have made. Their work continues to inspire future generations and move society towards a more inclusive and accepting world.

Subsection 4: Political and Legal Contributions

In this subsection, we will explore the significant political and legal contributions made by LGBTQ+ individuals throughout history. LGBTQ+ activists and advocates have played a crucial role in shaping laws, challenging societal norms, and fighting for the rights of their community. Their contributions have not only created more inclusive and equal societies but have also influenced the overall understanding and acceptance of diverse sexual orientations and gender identities.

Political Advocacy and Activism

One of the most remarkable political contributions by LGBTQ+ individuals is their work in political advocacy and activism. They have organized and mobilized on various fronts, championing for equal rights, protection, and recognition. LGBTQ+ organizations such as the Human Rights Campaign, GLAAD, and the LGBTQ Victory Fund have been at the forefront of these efforts.

These organizations have not only worked to support LGBTQ+ candidates in running for political office but have also effectively lobbied for the passage of LGBTQ+ inclusive legislation. The campaigning efforts by LGBTQ+ activists have been instrumental in the enactment of laws protecting against discrimination based on sexual orientation and gender identity. For example, the landmark Employment Non-Discrimination Act (ENDA) in the United States, which aims to protect LGBTQ+ individuals from workplace discrimination, is a direct result of their persistent advocacy.

Legal Challenges and Landmark Court Cases

LGBTQ+ individuals have also fought for their rights through the judicial system, bringing forward legal challenges that have reshaped the legal landscape and have had lasting effects. These court cases have played a crucial role in dismantling discriminatory laws and policies.

One such historic case is Lawrence v. Texas (2003) in the United States, where the Supreme Court struck down sodomy laws that criminalized consensual same-sex activity. This ruling was a turning point as it invalidated similar laws in other states and set the stage for further advancements in LGBTQ+ rights.

Another notable case is Obergefell v. Hodges (2015), also in the United States, where the Supreme Court recognized the constitutional right to same-sex marriage. This landmark ruling legalized same-sex marriage nationwide and marked a significant step towards equality for LGBTQ+ couples.

Internationally, legal challenges have also contributed to LGBTQ+ rights. For instance, the decriminalization of same-sex relationships in India in 2018 resulted from a successful legal challenge known as Navtej Singh Johar v. Union of India. This decision had a profound impact beyond India and inspired similar efforts around the world.

Progress in LGBTQ+ Representation

In addition to political advocacy and legal battles, LGBTQ+ individuals have made significant contributions to political representation. More LGBTQ+ individuals than ever before are running for and holding political office in many countries around the world. Their presence has brought diverse perspectives to policy-making and has given a voice to marginalized communities.

For example, in the United States, the election of Harvey Milk, the first openly gay elected official, to the San Francisco Board of Supervisors in 1977 paved the way for LGBTQ+ representation in politics. This milestone inspired many others to follow in his footsteps, working towards greater visibility and acceptance.

Furthermore, LGBTQ+ activists have been successful in influencing policy at federal, state, and local levels. This includes the implementation of hate crime legislation, the adoption of inclusive education policies, and the introduction of gender-neutral identification options.

Critical Issues and Future Challenges

While significant progress has been made, there are still critical issues and challenges that need to be addressed. LGBTQ+ individuals continue to face discrimination based on their sexual orientation or gender identity. Unequal access to healthcare, discrimination in employment, barriers to adoption and parenting, and the lack of comprehensive LGBTQ+ protection in many countries are some of the ongoing concerns.

Moving forward, it is essential to continue pushing for legislative reforms that protect LGBTQ+ individuals from discrimination in all aspects of life. Additionally, challenging societal attitudes and stereotypes through education and awareness campaigns remains crucial for achieving lasting change.

It is important to recognize and celebrate the political and legal contributions made by LGBTQ+ individuals. Their tireless efforts have paved the way for greater acceptance and equality, creating a more inclusive and diverse society for all. Through continued advocacy and activism, we can build on these achievements and strive for a future where LGBTQ+ individuals are fully embraced and protected.

Subsection 5: LGBTQ+ Influence in Fashion and Design

Fashion and design have always been powerful means of self-expression and creativity. Throughout history, LGBTQ+ individuals have played a significant role in shaping and revolutionizing these fields. Their unique perspectives and contributions have challenged traditional notions of gender, beauty, and style, leading to the emergence of diverse and inclusive fashion and design trends. In this section, we will explore the LGBTQ+ influence in fashion and design, highlighting their impact on aesthetics, representation, and societal norms.

The LGBTQ+ Aesthetic

The LGBTQ+ community has long been associated with breaking boundaries and defying social norms. This rebellious spirit has heavily influenced the aesthetics of fashion and design. LGBTQ+ individuals have introduced new silhouettes, color palettes, and concepts that challenge mainstream fashion industry standards.

One notable example is the androgynous style, which blurs the lines between traditionally masculine and feminine fashion. Icons like Marlene Dietrich and David Bowie embraced this style, inspiring generations to experiment with gender-neutral clothing. The androgynous aesthetic has since become an integral part of contemporary fashion, with designers such as Rei Kawakubo and Rick Owens pushing the boundaries of gender expression.

Furthermore, LGBTQ+ individuals have played a crucial role in the rise of streetwear culture. LGBTQ+ designers and influencers, such as Virgil Abloh and Tyler, the Creator, have infused streetwear with their unique perspectives, incorporating bold colors, graphic prints, and unconventional materials. This infusion has revitalized streetwear, making it more inclusive, diverse, and representative of LGBTQ+ identities.

Dismantling Binary Fashion

Historically, fashion has reinforced gender binaries, dictating how individuals should present themselves based on their assigned sex. However, the LGBTQ+

community has played a pivotal role in challenging these norms and advocating for more gender-inclusive fashion.

To address this, designers have introduced gender-neutral clothing lines, rejecting the notion of traditional masculine and feminine attire. These collections prioritize comfort, self-expression, and inclusivity, allowing individuals to dress in ways that align with their sense of identity rather than societal expectations.

Moreover, LGBTQ+ designers have championed the idea that fashion should be fluid and adaptable. They have created garments that can be worn by people of all genders, promoting a more inclusive and accessible fashion industry. This shift has not only empowered LGBTQ+ individuals but has also opened doors for greater acceptance and understanding of diverse gender identities.

Celebrating LGBTQ+ Representation

Representation matters, and LGBTQ+ individuals have used fashion and design as platforms for visibility and celebration of their identities. By using their work to showcase LGBTQ+ experiences, struggles, and triumphs, designers have fostered greater acceptance and understanding among wider audiences.

One notable example is the use of fashion campaigns to challenge heteronormativity and traditional beauty standards. LGBTQ+ designers and brands have showcased diverse models, including those who identify as LGBTQ+. This representation sends a powerful message, highlighting the beauty and uniqueness of LGBTQ+ individuals and breaking down societal norms around attractiveness.

Additionally, events like Pride parades and fashion shows have become significant platforms for LGBTQ+ designers to showcase their work and celebrate their identities. These events not only inspire creativity within the LGBTQ+ community but also promote acceptance and visibility on a larger scale.

Designing for Inclusivity

The LGBTQ+ influence in fashion and design goes beyond aesthetics and representation. LGBTQ+ individuals have also advocated for inclusivity and accessibility in design practices.

Designers have worked to create adaptive clothing that meets the unique needs of the LGBTQ+ community, such as gender-affirming garments for transgender and non-binary individuals. These designs prioritize comfort, functionality, and style, allowing individuals to express their identities authentically.

Furthermore, LGBTQ+ designers have been at the forefront of sustainable fashion movements. They have recognized the environmental impact of the fashion industry and have advocated for more ethical and eco-friendly practices. By promoting sustainable fashion, LGBTQ+ designers encourage consumers to make conscious choices that align with their values.

Taking Fashion Forward

The influence of LGBTQ+ individuals in fashion and design is undeniable. Their perspectives and contributions have shattered societal conventions, paving the way for a more inclusive and accepting industry.

As we move forward, it is crucial to continue celebrating LGBTQ+ voices, supporting LGBTQ+ designers, and fostering spaces where creativity and self-expression thrive. By embracing diversity and challenging norms, fashion and design can serve as powerful tools for societal change and empowerment.

Key Takeaways:

- LGBTQ+ individuals have played a significant role in shaping and revolutionizing fashion and design.
- The LGBTQ+ aesthetic challenges traditional fashion norms and embraces androgyny, streetwear, and diverse styles.
- LGBTQ+ designers have contributed to dismantling gender binaries by creating gender-neutral clothing lines.
- Fashion campaigns and events celebrate LGBTQ+ representation, challenging heteronormativity and traditional beauty standards.
- LGBTQ+ designers advocate for inclusivity and accessibility in design practices, creating adaptive clothing and promoting sustainable fashion.

Resources:

1. "Queer Style" by Valerie Steele
2. "Drag: The Complete Story" by Simon Doonan
3. "Fashion and its Social Agendas: Class, Gender, and Identity in Clothing" by Diana Crane
4. "One-Dimensional Queer" by Roderick Ferguson

5. "Gender Outlaws: The Next Generation" edited by Kate Bornstein and S. Bear Bergman

Remember, fashion and design are ever-evolving, and the LGBTQ+ community will continue to influence and shape these fields. By embracing diversity and challenging norms, we can create a more inclusive and representative industry that celebrates the rich tapestry of human identities.

Section 2: LGBTQ+ History and Movements

Subsection 1: Stonewall Riots and LGBTQ+ Rights Movement

The Stonewall Riots, which took place in June 1969, were a pivotal moment in the LGBTQ+ rights movement. The events that unfolded during those few days in New York City's Greenwich Village marked a turning point, igniting a renewed fight for equality and inspiring generations of activists.

Background

In the 1960s, homosexuality was still widely stigmatized, and discriminatory laws and practices were commonplace. LGBTQ+ individuals faced ongoing oppression, including police harassment, discrimination in employment, housing, and public services, and a general lack of acceptance and understanding from society at large.

The Stonewall Inn, a gay bar in New York City, was one of the few places where LGBTQ+ individuals could gather without fear of persecution. However, it was subjected to regular police raids, as law enforcement officials targeted establishments that served LGBTQ+ patrons.

The Riots

On the night of June 28, 1969, the Stonewall Inn was raided once again by police officers. However, this time, the LGBTQ+ community fought back. Frustrated and tired of the constant harassment and mistreatment, the patrons and community members resisted the police, leading to a series of violent clashes.

Marsha P. Johnson, a prominent transgender activist, and other LGBTQ+ leaders and allies played a crucial role in rallying the community and organizing resistance. The rioters, fighting for their dignity and rights, displayed unprecedented unity, resilience, and strength.

The protests lasted for several days, with LGBTQ+ individuals and allies flooding the streets around the Stonewall Inn. The riots forced the issue of

LGBTQ+ rights into the public consciousness and garnered significant media attention.

Impact and Legacy

The Stonewall Riots were a catalyst for the LGBTQ+ rights movement, sparking a wave of activism and organizing at local, national, and international levels. They set the stage for the formation of LGBTQ+ organizations, such as the Gay Liberation Front and the Gay Activists Alliance, which aimed to fight for equality and advocate for LGBTQ+ rights.

The riots also inspired the first LGBTQ+ pride marches, which took place on the anniversary of the riots in subsequent years. These marches provided a platform for LGBTQ+ individuals to publicly express their identity and demand equality.

Furthermore, the legacy of the Stonewall Riots extended beyond the LGBTQ+ community. The events served as a rallying cry for other marginalized groups and provided inspiration for their own struggles for rights and liberation.

Historical Context

To fully understand the significance of the Stonewall Riots, it is essential to recognize the broader historical context. The 1960s were marked by various social and political movements, including the civil rights movement, the feminist movement, and the anti-war movement.

The Stonewall Riots intersected with these movements, with LGBTQ+ activists forging alliances and finding common cause with other oppressed groups. This intersectionality played a vital role in shaping the direction and goals of the LGBTQ+ rights movement, as activists recognized the interconnectedness of struggles against discrimination and injustice.

Continued Struggle for LGBTQ+ Rights

While the Stonewall Riots marked a significant milestone, the fight for LGBTQ+ rights is far from over. Discrimination and prejudice still persist, and many LGBTQ+ individuals continue to face legal, social, and economic challenges.

Efforts to secure legal protections and advance LGBTQ+ rights have achieved notable successes, such as the decriminalization of homosexuality, the legalization of same-sex marriage in many countries, and legislation protecting LGBTQ+ individuals from discrimination. However, there is much work left to be done to ensure true equality and acceptance for all.

Resources and Further Reading

1. Carter, David. *Stonewall: The Riots That Sparked the Gay Revolution.* St. Martin's Press, 2004.

2. Duberman, Martin. *Stonewall.* Plume, 1994.

3. Teal, Donn. *The Gay Militants: How Gay Liberation Began in America, 1969-1971.* Abacus, 1995.

4. Johnson, David K. *The Lavender Scare: The Cold War Persecution of Gays and Lesbians in the Federal Government.* University of Chicago Press, 2004.

5. Chauncey, George. *Gay New York: Gender, Urban Culture, and the Making of the Gay Male World, 1890-1940.* Basic Books, 1995.

Discussion Questions

1. How did the Stonewall Riots contribute to the development of the LGBTQ+ rights movement?

2. In what ways did the Stonewall Riots intersect with other social and political movements of the 1960s?

3. What are some ongoing challenges faced by the LGBTQ+ community, and how can we continue to support and advocate for LGBTQ+ rights?

4. How has the legacy of the Stonewall Riots influenced the fight for LGBTQ+ rights in different parts of the world?

5. Why is it important to study and understand the history of LGBTQ+ activism and the Stonewall Riots in particular?

Subsection 2: LGBTQ+ Contributions to Literature and Film

In this subsection, we will explore the significant and groundbreaking contributions made by LGBTQ+ individuals in the realms of literature and film. LGBTQ+ writers, poets, filmmakers, and actors have played a vital role in shaping narratives, challenging societal norms, and advocating for greater acceptance and understanding. Their works have not only pushed boundaries but have also paved the way for more inclusive representations in these artistic mediums.

Literature

LGBTQ+ literature has a rich and diverse history that encompasses various genres, themes, and storytelling techniques. From classic works to contemporary pieces, the contributions of LGBTQ+ writers have both reflected and influenced societal perceptions of gender and sexuality. Let's delve into some significant aspects of LGBTQ+ literature.

1. Representation and Visibility One of the most powerful contributions of LGBTQ+ literature has been the representation and visibility it offers to individuals whose stories have often been marginalized or silenced. Through their writing, LGBTQ+ authors have amplified the voices and experiences of queer individuals, providing a platform for empathy, understanding, and connection.

For example, Audre Lorde's powerful poetry collection, "The Black Unicorn," explores intersectional identities, including being a black, lesbian woman. Lorde's work confronts the intersections of race, gender, and sexuality, highlighting the complexities of existence and challenging systemic oppressions.

2. Challenging Stereotypes and Norms LGBTQ+ literature has also been a catalyst for challenging stereotypes and societal norms surrounding gender and sexuality. By defying expectations and exploring unconventional narratives, LGBTQ+ authors have opened up conversations and fostered greater understanding.

Consider Virginia Woolf's iconic novel, "Orlando," which explores themes of gender fluidity and identity. Through the protagonist's transformation from a man to a woman, Woolf challenges rigid gender constructs and presents an alternative perspective on the fluidity of identity and desire.

3. Queer Theory and Critique LGBTQ+ literature has played a foundational role in the development of queer theory and critique. Scholars and literary critics have analyzed LGBTQ+ texts, examining themes of sexual identity, power dynamics, and social constructs of gender and sexuality. These critical frameworks have expanded the academic discourse surrounding LGBTQ+ literature and deepened our understanding of the complexities of queer experiences.

For instance, Judith Butler's influential book, "Gender Trouble," draws heavily from LGBTQ+ literature and interrogates the performative nature of gender. By challenging the binary norms of male and female, Butler's work has had a significant impact on literary theory and queer studies as a whole.

4. Coming-of-age Narratives Coming-of-age narratives have been a prominent theme within LGBTQ+ literature, representing the struggles and triumphs of young queer individuals as they navigate their identities and societal expectations. These stories provide a sense of affirmation, support, and guidance for LGBTQ+ youth, fostering a sense of belonging and acceptance.

A notable example is "Stone Butch Blues" by Leslie Feinberg, a classic novel that explores the life of a young butch lesbian named Jess. The book offers an authentic portrayal of the challenges faced by gender-nonconforming individuals and addresses the intersections of gender, class, and sexuality.

Film

Film has also been a powerful medium for LGBTQ+ individuals to tell their stories and challenge societal norms. LGBTQ+ filmmakers and actors have contributed immensely to cinema, both in front of and behind the camera. They have defied stereotypes, highlighted diverse experiences, and pushed for greater representation. Let's explore some key aspects of LGBTQ+ contributions to film.

1. **Representation on Screen** LGBTQ+ filmmakers have been pioneers in representing queer characters and stories on the big screen. By providing authentic and nuanced portrayals, they have shattered stereotypes and humanized LGBTQ+ experiences. These representations have helped to dispel prejudice and increase understanding and acceptance among audiences.

For example, the film "Moonlight," directed by Barry Jenkins, tells the story of a young black man exploring his sexuality amidst social and economic challenges. The film beautifully captures the struggles and triumphs of queer identity, and its critical acclaim demonstrates the power of LGBTQ+ narratives in film.

2. **Queer Cinema Movements** The emergence of queer cinema movements around the world has played a significant role in pushing boundaries and providing spaces for LGBTQ+ filmmakers to tell their stories. These movements have fostered artistic exploration, challenged societal norms, and provided platforms for LGBTQ+ representation that may have otherwise been marginalized or overlooked.

The New Queer Cinema movement in the 1990s, for instance, brought the work of LGBTQ+ filmmakers like Todd Haynes, Gus Van Sant, and Kimberly Peirce into the forefront. Films such as "Poison" and "Boys Don't Cry" tackled controversial subjects and broke new ground in terms of LGBTQ+ representation and storytelling.

3. **Film Festivals and LGBTQ+ Communities** Film festivals, such as the Sundance Film Festival and the Frameline Film Festival, have provided crucial

platforms for LGBTQ+ filmmakers to showcase their work and connect with audiences. These festivals celebrate and amplify LGBTQ+ voices, fostering a sense of community, and encouraging dialogue.

Additionally, the establishment of LGBTQ+ film festivals around the world has created spaces for marginalized voices and perspectives to be heard. These festivals provide opportunities for queer filmmakers to exhibit their work, network, and create a supportive community that nurtures artistic growth and innovation.

4. **Documentary and Activism** Documentary filmmaking has played a substantial role in raising awareness about LGBTQ+ issues and advocating for social change. Documentaries have provided a platform to showcase real-life stories, highlight activism, and expose the injustices faced by the LGBTQ+ community.

For instance, "Paris is Burning," directed by Jennie Livingston, offers an intimate look into New York City's drag ball culture, highlighting the experiences and challenges faced by gay and transgender people of color. The film not only celebrates the vibrancy of queer culture but also sheds light on the systemic discrimination and violence faced by these communities.

5. **Queer Theory and Film Studies** Similar to LGBTQ+ literature, the field of film studies has deeply engaged with queer theory, exploring the intersections of gender, sexuality, and representation in cinema. Scholars have analyzed LGBTQ+ films, deconstructing the narratives and challenging heteronormative ideologies.

An important text within this field is Richard Dyer's "The Matter of Images: Essays on Representation," which critically examines the representation of homosexuality in film. Dyer's work explores how LGBTQ+ characters have been historically constructed and interrogates the power dynamics at play in the cinematic portrayal of queer identities.

In conclusion, LGBTQ+ contributions to literature and film have been pivotal in reshaping narratives, challenging societal norms, and fostering greater understanding and acceptance of queer experiences. Through their writing, filmmaking, and acting, LGBTQ+ individuals have made profound and lasting impacts on these artistic realms, contributing to a more inclusive and diverse cultural landscape. Their works continue to inspire and pave the way for future generations to tell their stories with authenticity and pride.

Subsection 3: LGBTQ+ Impact in Sports and Athletics

Sports and athletics have always played a significant role in society, serving as a platform for competition, teamwork, and physical and mental well-being. For many years, LGBTQ+ individuals faced discrimination and exclusion in the world of sports. However, the LGBTQ+ community has made remarkable strides in breaking barriers and creating a more inclusive and accepting environment. This section explores the history, challenges, and triumphs of LGBTQ+ athletes, as well as the impact they have had on sports and athletics.

The Challenges Faced by LGBTQ+ Athletes

LGBTQ+ athletes have historically faced immense challenges and discrimination in sports and athletics. Homophobia, transphobia, and prejudice have created barriers to participation, acceptance, and equal treatment. Many LGBTQ+ athletes have had to hide their true identities for fear of backlash or exclusion. This secrecy often took a toll on their mental health and well-being, hindering their ability to perform at their best.

Furthermore, LGBTQ+ athletes have had to navigate the complexities of gender identity and sexual orientation within the context of sports. Policies and regulations around eligibility, gender segregation, and locker room accommodations have often been exclusionary and inflexible, making it difficult for transgender and non-binary athletes to compete comfortably.

Breaking Barriers and Creating Visibility

Despite the challenges they face, LGBTQ+ athletes have been instrumental in breaking down barriers and creating visibility within the sports world. By openly embracing their identities, these athletes have challenged societal norms and shattered stereotypes. Their courage and resilience have inspired a new generation of athletes to be their authentic selves and pursue their dreams without fear or prejudice.

One notable example is the journey of Caitlyn Jenner, a former Olympic decathlete. After transitioning in 2015, Jenner became a prominent advocate for transgender rights in sports. Her visibility and advocacy have sparked important conversations about inclusivity and fairness for transgender athletes.

Promoting Inclusivity and Equality

The impact of LGBTQ+ athletes goes beyond their individual achievements. They have brought attention to the need for inclusivity and equality in sports and have been at the forefront of advocating for policy changes and creating safe spaces for LGBTQ+ athletes.

Many sports organizations and governing bodies have implemented LGBTQ+ inclusion initiatives, such as creating LGBTQ+ resource groups, educational programs, and inclusive policies. These initiatives aim to foster a supportive and welcoming environment for LGBTQ+ athletes, coaches, and fans.

In addition to promoting inclusivity, LGBTQ+ athletes have also been instrumental in driving cultural change. Their visibility and success challenge societal prejudices and stereotypes while educating the broader public about the diversity within the LGBTQ+ community. This increased visibility helps combat discrimination and fosters greater acceptance in all areas of society.

Success Stories and Role Models

The success stories of LGBTQ+ athletes are numerous and inspiring. These athletes have achieved remarkable feats in their respective sports, proving that sexual orientation or gender identity does not limit athletic ability.

One such success story is that of Billie Jean King, a tennis icon and LGBTQ+ advocate. King's accomplishments on the court, including 39 Grand Slam titles, have made her one of the most influential athletes in history. Off the court, she has been a tireless advocate for gender equality and LGBTQ+ rights.

Another notable LGBTQ+ athlete is Megan Rapinoe, a soccer star and activist. Rapinoe's leadership on the field, including winning multiple World Cup titles, has been matched by her advocacy for LGBTQ+ rights and social justice.

These athletes, along with many others, serve as role models for the LGBTQ+ community, empowering future generations to pursue their passions and excel in sports without fear of discrimination.

Challenges and Potential Solutions

While progress has undoubtedly been made, challenges persist in ensuring full LGBTQ+ inclusion in sports and athletics. Some areas of concern include:

- Lack of comprehensive policies: Many sports organizations still lack clear policies regarding the inclusion of transgender and non-binary athletes. The development and implementation of inclusive policies are essential to ensure fair competition and participation for all athletes.

- Harassment and discrimination: LGBTQ+ athletes continue to face harassment and discrimination both on and off the field. Education and awareness campaigns can help address and eradicate these issues, fostering a culture of respect and acceptance.

- Representation and visibility: While progress has been made in terms of LGBTQ+ visibility in sports, more needs to be done. Highlighting the achievements and stories of LGBTQ+ athletes through media coverage and representation can help challenge stereotypes and inspire others.

By addressing these challenges and working collaboratively, sports organizations, athletes, fans, and the broader community can create a more inclusive and accepting environment for LGBTQ+ athletes in sports and athletics.

Conclusion

The impact of LGBTQ+ athletes in sports and athletics has been profound. Their courage, resilience, and achievements have played a significant role in breaking down barriers, creating visibility, and promoting inclusivity. Through their success stories and advocacy, they have inspired future generations to pursue their dreams without fear of discrimination. By continuing to address challenges and work towards more inclusive policies, we can build a more equitable and accepting sports community for all.

Subsection 4: Challenges and Progress in LGBTQ+ Rights

The struggle for LGBTQ+ rights has been a long and arduous journey. Over the years, the LGBTQ+ community has faced numerous challenges and obstacles in their fight for equality and acceptance. However, despite these challenges, there have also been significant advancements and progress in LGBTQ+ rights.

One significant challenge faced by the LGBTQ+ community is discrimination and prejudice. Many individuals and institutions continue to harbor homophobic and transphobic attitudes, leading to widespread discrimination in various aspects of life, including employment, housing, healthcare, and education. LGBTQ+ individuals often face higher rates of unemployment, homelessness, and mental health issues due to this discrimination.

Furthermore, laws and policies that discriminate against LGBTQ+ individuals still exist in many parts of the world. In some countries, same-sex relationships are criminalized, and LGBTQ+ individuals are at risk of arrest, imprisonment, and even death. In other countries, legal protections against discrimination based on sexual orientation and gender identity are lacking or inadequate.

Despite these challenges, there have been significant strides in LGBTQ+ rights globally. One major milestone is the decriminalization of homosexuality in many countries. This has been achieved through the tireless efforts of LGBTQ+ activists, organizations, and allies who have advocated for the repeal of discriminatory laws.

Another important area of progress is the recognition of same-sex marriage and civil unions. Many countries now legally recognize and grant equal marriage rights to same-sex couples, allowing them to enjoy the benefits and protections that come with marriage. This has been a significant step towards achieving equality and ending the stigmatization of LGBTQ+ relationships.

Furthermore, there has been an increased visibility and representation of the LGBTQ+ community in various aspects of society. LGBTQ+ individuals are now more visible in politics, entertainment, sports, and other fields, challenging stereotypes and breaking down barriers. This increased representation has helped to raise awareness and promote understanding of LGBTQ+ issues.

In recent years, there has also been a growing acceptance and awareness of transgender rights. Transgender individuals have been at the forefront of advocating for gender identity recognition and inclusive policies. Many countries have introduced legislation to protect the rights of transgender individuals, including legal gender recognition, access to healthcare, and protection against discrimination.

However, it is crucial to acknowledge that the fight for LGBTQ+ rights is far from over. Even in countries with legal protections, LGBTQ+ individuals still face significant challenges, including violence, harassment, and social exclusion. Additionally, transgender rights still lag behind, with many countries imposing restrictive requirements for legal gender recognition.

To address these challenges and continue progress in LGBTQ+ rights, it is necessary to implement comprehensive anti-discrimination laws and policies, improve education and awareness programs, and promote inclusivity in all aspects of society. It is crucial to challenge and dismantle the systemic biases and prejudices that perpetuate discrimination against LGBTQ+ individuals.

As allies and supporters, we can contribute to progress in LGBTQ+ rights by advocating for equal rights, challenging homophobia and transphobia, and creating inclusive environments in our communities. Everyone deserves to be treated with dignity, respect, and equality, regardless of their sexual orientation or gender identity.

In conclusion, the challenges faced by the LGBTQ+ community in their fight for rights and equality are significant. However, there have been significant advancements and progress in recent years. By continuing to raise awareness, advocate for change, and promote inclusive policies, we can work towards a future where LGBTQ+ individuals are fully accepted and embraced in all corners of society.

Chapter 4: Contributions of African and African American Communities

Section 1: Ancient African Civilizations and Contributions

Chapter 5: Contributions of African and African American Communities

Section 1: Ancient African Civilizations and Contributions

Subsection 1: African Philosophical Systems

African philosophy encompasses a rich and diverse range of thought systems that have existed on the continent for thousands of years. These philosophical systems, developed by various African cultures, have shaped the ways in which individuals understand the world around them, their place in society, and their relationships with others. In this subsection, we explore some key aspects of African philosophical systems and their contributions to human understanding.

Background

African philosophical systems have a long history dating back to ancient civilizations such as Egypt, Nubia, and Axum. These civilizations developed sophisticated belief systems and philosophical frameworks that continue to influence African societies today. It is important to note that African philosophy is not a monolithic entity, but rather a collection of diverse philosophical traditions that vary across different regions and cultural groups.

Ubuntu Philosophy

One prominent example of African philosophical thought is the concept of Ubuntu. Ubuntu, which originated in Southern Africa, is a worldview that places emphasis on the interconnectedness of all beings and the importance of communal harmony. The term "ubuntu" can be translated as "I am because we are" or "humanity towards others."

The Ubuntu philosophy promotes values such as compassion, empathy, and respect for others. It recognizes the interdependence between individuals and their communities, highlighting the need for cooperation and collective well-being. Ubuntu encourages individuals to strive for harmony and justice, and to recognize the inherent dignity and worth of every human being.

Oral Tradition and Philosophy

African philosophy is predominantly oral in nature, passed down through generations via storytelling, proverbs, and rituals. Oral tradition plays a crucial role in the transmission of philosophical concepts, as well as the preservation of cultural knowledge and historical narratives. Through storytelling, African philosophers impart wisdom, ethical principles, and lessons about human nature and the universe.

Oral tradition also serves as a platform for philosophical dialogue and debate within African communities. Through communal gatherings and social interactions, individuals engage in philosophical discussions, collectively constructing knowledge and understanding.

Epistemology and Ontology

African philosophical systems offer distinctive perspectives on epistemology (the study of knowledge) and ontology (the study of being). These perspectives challenge dominant Western philosophical paradigms and provide alternative frameworks for understanding reality.

Epistemologically, African philosophy emphasizes the importance of lived experience, intuition, and relational ways of knowing. It recognizes that knowledge can be acquired through direct engagement with the world and through interpersonal relationships. African epistemology values embodied knowledge, where individuals learn through active participation in their social and natural environments.

Ontologically, African philosophy emphasizes the interconnectedness and interdependence of all things. It rejects dualistic frameworks that separate mind and body, self and community, and human and non-human entities. Instead, African ontologies recognize the inherent interconnectedness and mutual dependence of all beings, shaping a holistic understanding of the world.

Contributions to Global Philosophy

African philosophical systems have made significant contributions to the overall landscape of global philosophy. They have challenged prevailing Eurocentric narratives and expanded the boundaries of philosophical inquiry. By centering African perspectives, these philosophical systems shed light on alternative ways of viewing the world and offer insights into questions of ethics, metaphysics, and epistemology.

Furthermore, African philosophy has significantly influenced other academic disciplines such as anthropology, sociology, and cultural studies. It provides valuable insights into the cultural practices, social structures, and belief systems of African communities.

Summary

African philosophical systems encompass a diverse range of thought traditions that have developed over thousands of years. These systems, such as Ubuntu philosophy, emphasize values of communal harmony, interconnectedness, and mutual respect. African philosophy challenges dominant Western paradigms, offering alternative perspectives on epistemology and ontology. It has made significant contributions to the global philosophical landscape, broadening our understanding of human existence and challenging prevailing Eurocentric narratives. By exploring African philosophical systems, we gain insights into the rich intellectual heritage and cultural contributions of African and African American communities.

Subsection 2: Architecture and Engineering Achievements

Architecture and engineering have played a remarkable role in African and African American history. This section explores the incredible accomplishments and contributions of African and African American communities in these fields. From ancient civilizations to modern innovations, the impact of their architectural and engineering achievements is undeniable.

Introduction to African Architectural Marvels

African architecture is rich and diverse, characterized by unique styles, techniques, and materials. The Pyramids of Egypt and Great Zimbabwe are iconic examples of African architectural marvels. The pyramids, built as tombs for pharaohs, showcase the advanced engineering skills of ancient Egyptians. In contrast, Great Zimbabwe represents the extraordinary stone masonry techniques used by the Shona people.

Influence on African American Architecture

African architectural traditions heavily influenced African American architecture in the United States. During the era of slavery, African captives brought their building and design knowledge, which was integrated into plantation architecture. The Gambrel-roofed houses and shotgun houses in the southern United States are rooted in African architectural styles.

Innovative Building Techniques

African builders developed innovative techniques to construct structures that have withstood the test of time. One such technique is the use of mud bricks and adobe construction. Mud-brick structures, like the Great Mosque of Djenné in Mali, showcase intricate designs and demonstrate the strength and durability of this building method.

Engineering Marvels

African engineers displayed their ingenuity in the design and construction of elaborate water management systems. The ancient Egyptians, for instance, implemented sophisticated irrigation systems like the Qanat, which allowed for efficient farming in arid regions. Similarly, the construction of the intricate terraced fields in the Ethiopian highlands exemplifies advanced engineering techniques.

Impactful Structures in African American Communities

The architectural accomplishments of African American communities are showcased in various structures across the United States. The Tuskegee Institute's campus buildings, designed by African American architect Robert Robinson

Taylor, serve as lasting symbols of African American excellence in architecture. Additionally, the Harlem Renaissance period gave rise to numerous architecturally significant buildings, including the Savoy Ballroom and the Apollo Theater in New York City.

Modern Contributions in Architecture and Engineering

African and African American architects continue to shape the modern world with their innovative designs and contributions. Prominent architects like Philip Freelon and David Adjaye have left indelible marks on the architectural landscape with their award-winning designs, including the National Museum of African American History and Culture in Washington, D.C., and the Smithsonian National Museum of African American History in Chicago.

Unconventional Approach: Sustainable Architecture

Sustainable architecture is an emerging field that combines innovative design principles with environmentally friendly practices. African and African American architects have been at the forefront of this movement, incorporating sustainable building materials, passive design strategies, and renewable energy systems into their projects. Examples include the Zeitz Museum of Contemporary Art Africa in Cape Town, which repurposed a historic grain silo into a sustainable cultural hub.

Conclusion

The architectural and engineering achievements of African and African American communities have had a profound impact on the world. From ancient African civilizations to modern-day innovations, their contributions have transformed the built environment. By recognizing and celebrating their achievements, we not only honor their legacy but also inspire future generations of architects and engineers to continue pushing the boundaries of creativity and technical excellence.

Subsection 3: African Mathematical and Astronomical Knowledge

Africa has a rich history of mathematical and astronomical knowledge that is often overlooked in traditional narratives of global history. This section aims to shed light on the contributions made by African cultures in these fields, showcasing their innovative ideas and advanced understanding of mathematics and astronomy.

Historical Background

Mathematics and astronomy have deep roots in African civilizations, dating back thousands of years. African mathematicians and astronomers developed sophisticated systems and concepts to explain natural phenomena and solve practical problems. These advancements were nurtured in various regions across the continent, including ancient Egypt, Nubia, Ghana, Mali, and Ethiopia.

Mathematical Achievements

African mathematical knowledge encompassed various areas, including arithmetic, geometry, algebra, and numerical systems. One prominent example is the ancient Egyptians' mastery of arithmetic and geometry. They developed a decimal system based on powers of ten, enabling efficient calculations and sophisticated architectural designs. The construction of pyramids and temples stands as a testament to their advanced understanding of geometry.

In West Africa, the empire of Mali flourished during the 14th century. The mathematicians of Mali developed an intricate numerical system using cowrie shells, allowing them to perform complex calculations. This system, known as the "Malian algebra," laid the foundation for advanced trade and commerce within the empire.

Astronomical Knowledge

Astronomy held significant importance in many African cultures, guiding agricultural practices, religious rituals, and navigation. Ancient Egyptians were renowned for their celestial observations and the development of a calendar based on the cycles of the sun and the Nile River. Their understanding of astronomy greatly influenced their agricultural practices and planning of religious festivals.

In Ethiopia, the ancient kingdom of Axum developed an impressive astronomical system. They accurately predicted celestial events, including lunar and solar eclipses, through observations and sophisticated mathematical calculations. This knowledge played a crucial role in their religious practices and governance.

Indigenous African cultures also had advanced knowledge of the stars and constellations. The Dogon people of Mali, for instance, possessed an in-depth understanding of the Sirius star system, including the existence of its companion star. This knowledge, passed down through generations, challenged Western scientific understanding when it was revealed in the 20th century.

Applications and Cultural Significance

African mathematical and astronomical knowledge had practical applications in various fields. The advanced architectural designs of ancient Egypt utilized geometric concepts and precise calculations. African numerals and numerical systems facilitated trade, commerce, and record-keeping.

Moreover, African mathematical and astronomical systems were intertwined with cultural and spiritual beliefs. The alignment of sacred sites with celestial events and constellations played a crucial role in religious rituals and social ceremonies. Understanding these connections enhances our appreciation of African cultures' rich heritage.

Modern Perspectives and Recognition

The contributions of African mathematics and astronomy are gradually gaining recognition and appreciation in the modern world. Scholars and researchers are actively working to reconstruct and preserve ancient African mathematical systems, as well as studying indigenous knowledge systems still practiced today.

In contemporary Africa, efforts are being made to revive and integrate traditional mathematical and astronomical knowledge into educational curricula. This allows younger generations to reconnect with their cultural roots and appreciate the depth and significance of their ancestors' contributions.

Challenges and Future Directions

Despite the growing recognition, there are challenges in exploring and promoting African mathematical and astronomical knowledge. Limited access to historical documents and resources hinders comprehensive research. Furthermore, the Eurocentric biases prevalent in academic disciplines have often overshadowed Africa's contributions.

To address these challenges, it is crucial to foster interdisciplinary collaborations between African scholars, archaeologists, astronomers, and mathematicians. By combining traditional knowledge with modern research methodologies, a more holistic understanding of African mathematical and astronomical heritage can be achieved.

Conclusion

African mathematical and astronomical knowledge showcases the ingenuity and intellectual achievements of diverse African cultures throughout history. From the advanced arithmetic and geometric systems of ancient Egypt and Mali to the intricate astronomical observations of Ethiopia and the Dogon people, Africa's contributions have shaped human understanding of the cosmos and real-world applications of mathematics. Recognizing and celebrating these contributions not only enriches our knowledge but also highlights the necessity of diverse perspectives in the global narrative of human achievement.

Subsection 4: African Dietary and Agricultural Practices

Agriculture has always played a significant role in human civilization, providing the foundation for food security and societal development. In Africa, a rich diversity of dietary and agricultural practices has emerged over centuries, shaped by the continent's unique climatic conditions, geographical features, and cultural diversity. In this subsection, we will explore the fascinating world of African dietary and agricultural practices, highlighting their importance, techniques, and impact on global food systems.

Background: Sustainable Agriculture in Africa

The agricultural practices developed by African communities are deeply rooted in sustainability and resilience. Rather than relying on large-scale monocultures, African farmers have adopted innovative methods that maximize yields while preserving the surrounding ecosystems. These practices have strengthened the resilience of African communities, allowing them to adapt to the challenges posed by climate change and other environmental factors.

Traditional African Crops and Farming Techniques

African agriculture is characterized by the cultivation of a diverse range of crops that are well-suited to the local climate and soil conditions. These crops include staples such as maize, millet, sorghum, and rice, as well as nutrient-rich vegetables like cowpea, yam, and okra. Each crop has its own unique farming techniques that have been refined over generations.

For example, the cultivation of maize often involves intercropping with legumes to increase soil fertility and reduce pest infestations. Farmers in West Africa have also developed a technique called "push-pull farming," where they intercrop maize with Desmodium, a plant that repels pests, while simultaneously planting Napier grass as a trap crop to attract and control pests.

Water Management and Irrigation Systems

African farmers have devised effective water management and irrigation systems to overcome the challenges of water scarcity in many regions. One such system is called "zai," which involves digging small planting holes during the dry season and adding manure or crop residues to enhance water retention in the soil. This technique increases soil moisture, leading to greater crop yields and improved soil fertility.

Additionally, African farmers have utilized a method known as "bunds" to conserve water and prevent soil erosion. Bunds are small ridges or embankments constructed across slopes to slow down the flow of water, allowing it to infiltrate the soil and reduce runoff. This technique helps retain moisture in the fields, especially during periods of drought.

Integration of Livestock and Crop Farming

African farmers have long recognized the benefits of integrating livestock and crop farming systems. Livestock play a crucial role in providing traction for plowing, manure for fertilization, and a source of protein-rich food. This integration increases agricultural productivity while minimizing the negative environmental impacts associated with intensive livestock farming.

For example, in some parts of Africa, farmers practice a technique called "agro-pastoralism" where livestock are allowed to graze on crop residues and fallow fields after harvest. This helps control weeds, adds organic matter to the soil, and improves nutrient cycling.

Promoting African Dietary Diversity

African dietary practices are characterized by a wide variety of nutrient-rich foods, contributing to a balanced and healthy diet. Traditional African diets often include a combination of staples, legumes, fruits, vegetables, and indigenous plant species. This diversity not only provides essential nutrients but also helps to reduce malnutrition and promote overall well-being.

Efforts are underway to promote and preserve African dietary diversity. Local communities, alongside researchers and NGOs, are working together to document and promote traditional African recipes, which showcase the use of indigenous crops and cooking techniques. By revitalizing traditional foods, African communities can enhance food security, improve nutrition, and support local agriculture.

Challenges and Opportunities

While African agricultural practices have proven their resilience over centuries, they face several challenges in the modern world. Climate change, population growth, and limited access to resources and markets pose significant obstacles to sustainable agriculture in Africa.

However, there are also opportunities for innovation and growth. Increased investment in agricultural research and development, the adoption of modern technologies, and the promotion of sustainable farming practices can help African farmers overcome these challenges. Furthermore, partnerships between governments, local communities, and international organizations can facilitate knowledge-sharing and the exchange of best practices.

Conclusion

African dietary and agricultural practices are a testament to the ingenuity and wisdom of the continent's farming communities. By recognizing and valuing these practices, we can develop a more inclusive and sustainable approach to global food systems. Embracing traditional knowledge, supporting small-scale farmers, and promoting agricultural diversity will not only contribute to food security but also enable us to address the pressing challenges of our time. Let us celebrate the rich legacy of African agriculture and learn from its lessons for a more prosperous and sustainable future.

Subsection 5: African Art and Cultural Expressions

African art and cultural expressions have a rich history that spans thousands of years. From ancient sculptures and masks to contemporary paintings and performances, African art has captivated audiences around the world. In this section, we will explore the various forms of African art and the cultural significance they hold.

Understanding African Art

African art is characterized by its diversity and the connection it has to the spiritual and cultural beliefs of different African communities. It encompasses a wide range of forms, including sculpture, painting, textiles, ceramics, jewelry, music, dance, and theater. Each artistic expression is deeply rooted in the traditions, rituals, and stories of African culture.

One notable aspect of African art is its emphasis on communal and functional purposes. Many artworks serve a specific function within the community, such as masks used in rituals or sculptures that depict ancestral figures. Art is seen as a means of connecting with the spiritual realm and often plays a significant role in ceremonies and social gatherings.

Traditional African Sculpture

Sculpture is one of the most prominent forms of African art, dating back thousands of years. Traditional African sculptures are known for their expressive and abstract forms, reflecting the diverse cultures and beliefs of the continent. These sculptures often depict human figures, animals, or mythical creatures, and are made from materials such as wood, bronze, terracotta, or ivory.

One prominent example of traditional African sculpture is the Benin Bronzes from Nigeria. These intricately detailed bronze sculptures were created by the Edo people in the Kingdom of Benin and depict royalty, warriors, and deities. They were primarily used to decorate the royal palace and serve as symbols of power and prestige.

Contemporary African Art

While traditional African art continues to thrive, contemporary African artists have also made significant contributions to the art world. Contemporary African art encompasses a wide range of mediums and styles, often incorporating modern techniques and materials.

One influential contemporary African artist is El Anatsui from Ghana. He is known for his large-scale sculptures made from recycled materials, such as bottle caps and metal scraps. His works explore themes of consumerism, globalization, and African history, creating visually stunning and thought-provoking pieces.

Another notable artist is Marlene Dumas from South Africa. She is renowned for her figurative paintings, which often tackle themes of identity, race, and politics. Her powerful and emotive portrayals have garnered international acclaim, shedding light on the complexities of the African experience.

The Significance of African Art

African art holds great significance within African communities and has also gained recognition globally for its cultural value and artistic prowess. It serves as a visual language, conveying stories, beliefs, and histories across generations. Moreover, it provides a means of preserving and celebrating African cultural heritage.

Beyond its cultural significance, African art has also influenced and inspired artists worldwide. Many Western artists, such as Pablo Picasso and Henri Matisse, were captivated by the expressive forms and bold designs of African art, leading to the emergence of the modern art movement known as "Primitivism."

Preserving African Art

Preserving African art is essential to safeguarding cultural heritage and ensuring its continued appreciation and understanding. However, many African artworks have been subject to looting, illegal trade, and unethical collection practices. Efforts are underway to repatriate stolen artifacts and establish proper protocols for the ethical acquisition and display of African art.

Museums, galleries, and cultural institutions play a crucial role in showcasing African art to wider audiences and fostering cross-cultural understanding. They provide spaces for African artists to exhibit their works and support initiatives that promote the preservation and documentation of African art forms.

Exploring African Art: An Exercise

To deepen your understanding of African art, take a moment to explore the work of a contemporary African artist. Choose an artist whose works resonate with you or pique your interest. Research their background, artistic style, and the themes they explore in their art.

Write a short reflection on how this artist's work embodies African cultural expressions and how it challenges or expands your understanding of African art. Consider the artist's use of materials, techniques, and visual elements in conveying their message. Discuss how their art reflects broader social, political, or historical contexts within Africa or the African diaspora.

By engaging with the works of contemporary African artists, you can gain a deeper appreciation for the vibrancy and diversity of African art and its lasting impact on the global art scene.

Further Resources

If you would like to explore African art further, here are some recommended resources:

- "African Art: A Century at the Brooklyn Museum" by Marian L. Miller and Christa Clarke

- "African Art and Agency in the Workshop" edited by Sidney Littlefield Kasfir
- "African Art in Detail" by Chris Spring
- "The Power of African Art" by Tom Phillips
- Websites such as the Metropolitan Museum of Art's *Art of Africa*, the Smithsonian National Museum of African Art, and the African Art Museum of Maryland provide online collections and comprehensive information on different African art forms.

These resources offer valuable insights into the history, aesthetics, and cultural significance of African art, allowing you to delve deeper into this fascinating and multifaceted field.

In conclusion, African art and cultural expressions encompass a wide array of forms that reflect the rich and diverse traditions of the continent. From traditional sculptures rooted in spirituality to contemporary artworks challenging social norms, African art continues to captivate and inspire audiences worldwide. By appreciating and understanding African art, we gain a deeper appreciation for the cultural heritage and artistic contributions of African communities.

Section 2: Influence of African American Culture in the United States

Subsection 1: African American Music Traditions

African American music traditions have had a profound impact on American culture and have significantly influenced various genres of music throughout history. The rich and diverse heritage of African American music reflects the struggles, triumphs, and creative expressions of African Americans in the United States. This subsection explores the historical origins, key musical styles, significant musicians, and the lasting legacy of African American music traditions.

Origins and Influences

African American music has deep roots in African musical traditions brought to the Americas during the transatlantic slave trade. Enslaved Africans preserved their cultural identity through music, adapting their traditional rhythms, melodies, and instrumentation to new circumstances. Elements such as call and response, polyrhythms, improvisation, and communal participation became fundamental aspects of African American musical expressions.

The fusion of African musical traditions with European musical styles during slavery and the post-emancipation period further shaped African American music. This blending gave rise to unique genres such as spirituals, work songs, and blues, which provided a means of communication, spiritual solace, and artistic expression in response to the hardships endured by African Americans.

Key Musical Styles

1. **Spirituals:** Spirituals were religious songs that originated in the African American slave communities. They often incorporated biblical themes and encoded messages of hope, liberation, and resistance. Spirituals were characterized by their expressive vocal delivery, vocal harmonies, and rhythmic patterns. Notable spirituals include "Swing Low, Sweet Chariot" and "Wade in the Water."

2. **Blues:** The blues, born in the Mississippi Delta region, is a genre characterized by its melancholic lyrics, distinctive chord progressions, and expressive use of guitar. It served as a foundation for many other genres, such as jazz, rock 'n' roll, and rhythm and blues. Influential blues musicians include Robert Johnson, B.B. King, and Muddy Waters.

3. **Jazz:** Jazz, often referred to as America's classical music, emerged in the early 20th century and incorporated elements of African music, European classical music, and African American musical traditions. Jazz is known for its improvisation, syncopation, complex harmonies, and swing feel. Legendary jazz musicians include Louis Armstrong, Duke Ellington, and Ella Fitzgerald.

4. **Gospel:** Gospel music, rooted in African American churches, is characterized by its energetic and uplifting performances. It combines Christian hymns with African musical elements, featuring powerful vocal solos, harmonies, and hand-clapping rhythms. Influential gospel artists include Mahalia Jackson, Thomas A. Dorsey, and Aretha Franklin.

5. **R&B/Soul:** Rhythm and blues (R&B) and soul music evolved from the blues and gospel traditions. R&B became popular during the mid-20th century, featuring a combination of jazz, blues, and gospel elements. Soul music, influenced by R&B, added a greater emphasis on emotional expression and personal storytelling. Notable R&B and soul artists include Sam Cooke, Ray Charles, and Stevie Wonder.

Significant Musicians

African American music traditions have produced numerous influential musicians who have left an indelible mark on the world of music. Here are a few notable figures:

1. **Louis Armstrong:** A jazz legend and trumpeter, Louis Armstrong revolutionized jazz improvisation and became one of the most influential musicians of the 20th century.
2. **Aretha Franklin:** Known as the "Queen of Soul," Aretha Franklin's powerful voice and emotional delivery made her one of the greatest singers in music history.
3. **Miles Davis:** A pioneering jazz trumpeter, composer, and band leader, Miles Davis consistently pushed the boundaries of jazz and reinvented himself throughout his career.
4. **Jimi Hendrix:** Considered one of the greatest guitarists of all time, Jimi Hendrix revolutionized rock music with his innovative playing style and mesmerizing performances.
5. **Beyoncé:** As a contemporary artist, Beyoncé has redefined pop, R&B, and soul music, using her platform to celebrate African American culture and advocate for social justice.

Legacy and Evolution

African American music traditions continue to shape and influence modern music across various genres. The impact of African American music can be seen in the widespread adoption of African rhythms, blues progressions, and gospel-inspired vocals in popular music. Modern artists often draw inspiration from the rich heritage of African American music, paying homage to its origins while incorporating their unique artistic vision.

Furthermore, African American music has played a crucial role in empowering marginalized communities, fostering social change, and raising awareness about systemic injustices. From songs of protest during the civil rights movement to the ongoing use of music as a tool for activism, African American musicians have used their music to challenge societal norms and advocate for equality.

In conclusion, African American music traditions are a testament to the resilience, creativity, and cultural contributions of African Americans throughout history. By recognizing and celebrating the immense impact of African American musicians, we acknowledge the transformative power of music and continue the legacy of these influential traditions.

Summary

- African American music traditions originated from African musical traditions brought by enslaved Africans and evolved through fusion with European musical styles. - Key musical styles include spirituals, blues, jazz, gospel, and R&B/soul. - Notable musicians include Louis Armstrong, Aretha Franklin, Miles Davis, Jimi Hendrix, and Beyoncé. - African American music has had a lasting legacy, influencing various genres and playing a crucial role in social change and empowerment.

Key Terms

- Spirituals - Blues - Jazz - Gospel - R&B/Soul - Louis Armstrong - Aretha Franklin - Miles Davis - Jimi Hendrix - Beyoncé

Further Reading

- Burnim, M. (Ed.). (2006). *The African American Music Trail in North Carolina*. University of North Carolina Press. - Southern, E. (1997). *The Music of Black Americans: A History*. W. W. Norton & Company. - Floyd, S. (2001). *The Power of Black Music: Interpreting Its History from Africa to the United States*. Oxford University Press.

Subsection 2: African American Literature and Intellectual Movements

African American literature and intellectual movements have played a crucial role in shaping American culture and challenging societal norms. From the early slave narratives to the Harlem Renaissance and beyond, African American writers and thinkers have made significant contributions to literature, philosophy, and social activism. In this section, we will explore the rich history and impact of African American literature and intellectual movements.

The Power of African American Literature

African American literature emerged as a powerful form of expression during slavery and continues to thrive today. It serves as a medium to explore the African American experience, address social issues, and celebrate cultural heritage. The works of African American writers have provided insights into the struggles of black Americans, showcasing their resilience, strength, and achievements.

One prominent figure in African American literature is Frederick Douglass, who wrote his autobiography, "Narrative of the Life of Frederick Douglass, an American Slave" in 1845. Douglass's narrative exposed the brutality of slavery and became a rallying cry for the abolitionist movement. His eloquent language and powerful storytelling not only educated readers about the horrors of slavery but also humanized the experiences of enslaved individuals.

Another pivotal figure in African American literature is Zora Neale Hurston, whose novel "Their Eyes Were Watching God" (1937) explored themes of race, gender, and identity. Hurston's vibrant storytelling and portrayal of black rural life provided a counter-narrative to prevailing stereotypes. Her work challenged societal expectations and gave voice to African American women.

In recent years, writers like Ta-Nehisi Coates and Jesmyn Ward have gained critical acclaim, capturing the contemporary African American experience with their thought-provoking and emotional narratives. Their works delve into themes of racial injustice, systemic racism, and the complexities of identity.

The Harlem Renaissance

The Harlem Renaissance, spanning the 1920s to the mid-1930s, was a vibrant cultural and intellectual movement centered in Harlem, New York City. It showcased the artistic and literary genius of African Americans and challenged prevailing racial stereotypes. The movement encompassed various art forms, including literature, poetry, visual arts, music, and theater.

One of the seminal figures of the Harlem Renaissance was Langston Hughes, a poet, novelist, and playwright. Hughes's poetry, such as "The Weary Blues" and "Harlem (Dream Deferred)," gave voice to the African American experience, capturing both the joys and struggles of black life. His work often incorporated jazz rhythms and colloquial language, creating a unique form of artistic expression.

The Harlem Renaissance also saw the rise of the literary magazine *The Crisis*, founded by W.E.B. Du Bois. The magazine provided a platform for African American writers and intellectuals to share their works and address social issues. Through literature and intellectual discourse, the Harlem Renaissance challenged societal norms, promoted racial pride, and fostered a sense of community among African Americans.

Intellectual Movements and Thinkers

Alongside literature, African American intellectuals have made significant contributions to philosophical and social movements. One such movement is the Black Arts Movement, which emerged in the 1960s and 1970s. It sought to create an artistic and cultural renaissance within the African American community, encouraging self-determination and challenging Eurocentrism.

Amiri Baraka, formerly known as LeRoi Jones, was a pivotal figure in the Black Arts Movement. His play "Dutchman" addressed themes of racial and sexual politics, confronting white supremacy and advocating for black liberation. Baraka's work pushed the boundaries of artistic expression, merging poetry, drama, and political activism.

Another influential thinker is Angela Davis, an activist, scholar, and author who played a key role in various civil rights and feminist movements. Davis's writings have addressed issues of race, gender, and class, highlighting the intersections of oppression. Her work continues to inspire and challenge contemporary social justice movements.

Recognizing the Complexity

It is essential to acknowledge that African American literature and intellectual movements are diverse and encompass a wide range of perspectives and genres. From poetry and fiction to non-fiction and critical theory, African American writers and thinkers have contributed to various aspects of intellectual discourse.

However, it is important to avoid essentializing or homogenizing African American experiences. Diversity within the African American community exists, and literature and intellectual movements reflect this complexity. African American writers and thinkers offer different perspectives on identity, history, and social issues, enriching our understanding of the African American experience.

Conclusion

African American literature and intellectual movements have played a vital role in shaping American culture and challenging societal norms. From the powerful narratives of Frederick Douglass to the vibrant artistic expression of the Harlem Renaissance and the thought-provoking works of contemporary writers, African American contributions have enriched the literary and intellectual landscape of the United States.

By exploring the diverse voices and perspectives within African American literature and intellectual movements, we gain a deeper understanding of the African American experience, challenge prevailing stereotypes, and work towards a more inclusive and equitable society.

Subsection 3: African American Contributions to Civil Rights Movements

The Civil Rights Movement in the United States was a significant period of social and political activism, primarily aimed at addressing racial segregation and discrimination against African Americans. African Americans played a crucial role in this movement, making important contributions that led to significant progress in the fight for equality and justice. In this section, we will explore the key contributions of African Americans to the Civil Rights Movement and the impact they had on shaping a more inclusive society.

Challenging Segregation Laws

One of the pivotal moments in the Civil Rights Movement was the challenge to segregation laws. African American activists like Rosa Parks, who famously refused to give up her seat on a segregated bus in Montgomery, Alabama, sparked a wave of protests against racial segregation. The Montgomery Bus Boycott, led by Dr. Martin Luther King Jr., was a successful demonstration of nonviolent resistance that ultimately resulted in a Supreme Court ruling declaring segregation on buses unconstitutional. This victory inspired other activists and set a precedent for future legal challenges to discriminatory laws.

Leadership and Organizing

African American leaders emerged during the Civil Rights Movement, providing guidance and mobilizing communities to work towards change. Dr. Martin Luther King Jr., as one of the most prominent figures, advocated for peaceful protests and nonviolent resistance as effective means of achieving civil rights. His powerful speeches, such as the famous "I Have a Dream" speech, galvanized millions of Americans and helped to shape public opinion on racial equality.

Additionally, other leaders like Malcolm X and the Black Panther Party adopted more militant approaches, challenging the status quo and demanding immediate and radical change. These leaders represented different strategies and ideologies within the movement, reflecting the diversity of thought and the range of tactics employed by African Americans in their pursuit of civil rights.

Student Activism

African American students played a crucial role in the Civil Rights Movement, organizing sit-ins, protests, and marches to challenge racial segregation in schools and public spaces. The Greensboro sit-ins in 1960, where four African American college students staged a peaceful protest at a segregated lunch counter, sparked a wave of similar demonstrations across the country. These student-led actions brought national attention to the injustices of segregation and invigorated the movement.

Student activists also played a significant role in voter registration drives, helping to mobilize African Americans to exercise their right to vote and participate in the democratic process. Their efforts contributed to the passing of the Voting Rights Act of 1965, which aimed to eliminate discriminatory voting practices and protect minority voting rights.

Legal Strategies

African American lawyers and legal organizations played a vital role in the fight for civil rights. Thurgood Marshall, the first African American Supreme Court Justice, and the NAACP Legal Defense Fund were instrumental in challenging segregation in the courts. Through strategic litigation, they worked to dismantle the legal framework supporting racial discrimination.

Landmark cases such as Brown v. Board of Education (1954), which declared racial segregation in public schools unconstitutional, marked a turning point in the fight against segregation. These legal victories not only struck down discriminatory laws but also paved the way for wider social change by challenging deeply entrenched racist practices.

Legacy and Continuing Struggles

The contributions of African Americans to the Civil Rights Movement have had a lasting impact on American society. The legislative achievements, such as the Civil Rights Act of 1964 and the Voting Rights Act of 1965, are significant milestones in the ongoing struggle for equality. These laws provided legal protections against racial discrimination and established mechanisms for ensuring equal access to education, employment, and public facilities.

However, it is important to recognize that the fight for civil rights is not over. Systemic racism continues to persist in various forms, and African Americans, along with other marginalized communities, still face social and economic disparities. The legacies of the Civil Rights Movement serve as a reminder that the struggle for equality requires ongoing vigilance and collective action.

Resources

To further explore the contributions of African Americans to the Civil Rights Movement, here are some recommended resources:

- *The Autobiography of Malcolm X* by Malcolm X and Alex Haley
- *Eyes on the Prize: America's Civil Rights Years, 1954-1965* by Juan Williams
- *March: Book One, Two, and Three* by John Lewis, Andrew Aydin, and Nate Powell
- *The Fire Next Time* by James Baldwin
- *Parting the Waters: America in the King Years 1954-63* by Taylor Branch

These resources provide valuable insights into the experiences, struggles, and triumphs of African Americans during the Civil Rights Movement and can deepen your understanding of this critical period in American history.

Exercise

Think about a contemporary social justice issue that resonates with you. Consider how the strategies and contributions of African American activists during the Civil Rights Movement can inspire and inform activism today. Write a short reflection discussing the parallels between past struggles for civil rights and the ongoing fight for justice in our society.

Subsection 4: African American Influence in Sports and Pop Culture

African American athletes and entertainers have made significant contributions to sports and pop culture, shaping the landscape and influencing generations. From breaking records to challenging social norms, their trailblazing achievements have left an indelible mark on society. In this section, we will explore the rich history of African Americans in sports and their impact on popular culture.

Breaking Barriers: Pioneers in Sports

African Americans faced numerous obstacles and discrimination in their pursuit of sports excellence. However, their determination and outstanding abilities shattered racial barriers, allowing them to compete at the highest level and redefine the possibilities for future generations.

One prominent figure who revolutionized American sports is Jackie Robinson. In 1947, Robinson became the first African American to play in Major League Baseball, breaking the color barrier. His courage and resilience paved the way for other African American baseball players, significantly transforming the game and challenging racial segregation.

In addition to Robinson, many other African American athletes overcame adversity to achieve greatness. In track and field, Jesse Owens showcased his unparalleled speed and agility by winning four gold medals at the 1936 Olympics, held in Nazi Germany. Owens' accomplishments not only showcased his exceptional talent but also defied Hitler's Aryan supremacist ideals.

Basketball legend Michael Jordan is another iconic figure who transcended racial boundaries. With his incredible athleticism and unmatched skills, Jordan became a cultural phenomenon. He not only dominated the court but also became a global brand and an inspiration for aspiring athletes worldwide.

Cultural Impact: Heroes and Icons

African American athletes and entertainers have become heroes and icons, capturing the hearts and imaginations of people around the world. Their achievements have transcended the realm of sports, resonating deeply within popular culture.

Muhammad Ali, considered one of the greatest boxers of all time, transcended the sport with his charisma, courage, and activism. Beyond his exceptional boxing skills, Ali used his platform to speak out against social injustice and civil rights violations, making a lasting impact in the struggle for equality.

In the realm of music, African American artists have profoundly influenced popular culture. From the soulful voices of Aretha Franklin and Stevie Wonder to the groundbreaking lyrics of Tupac Shakur and Beyoncé, African American musicians have created anthems that resonate with diverse audiences. Their music has not only entertained but also served as a powerful catalyst for change and self-expression.

In the film industry, notable African American actors and directors have defied stereotypes and challenged the status quo. Visionaries like Sidney Poitier and Spike Lee paved the way for greater representation and diversity on screen, telling stories that had long been ignored or marginalized. Their contributions have reshaped the way audiences perceive race and identity in cinema.

Social Impact: Inspiring Generations

African American athletes and entertainers have inspired generations of individuals, not only within their respective communities but also across racial and cultural boundaries. Their success stories serve as a source of empowerment and motivation, illustrating the potential for greatness in the face of adversity.

The achievements of African American athletes have had a profound impact on young aspiring athletes. Seeing individuals who look like them achieve excellence in sports has encouraged many to pursue their dreams and overcome barriers. The success of athletes like Serena Williams and LeBron James continues to inspire a diverse range of individuals, transcending the boundaries of race and instilling a belief in the power of perseverance.

Similarly, African American entertainers have helped shape cultural identity and inspire creativity. From the vibrant fashion statements of Rihanna to the thought-provoking lyrics of Kendrick Lamar, these artists have become cultural ambassadors, advocating for social change and challenging societal norms.

Current Challenges and Future Outlook

Despite the progress made, African Americans in sports and pop culture still face significant challenges. Systemic racism, limited representation, and unequal access to resources continue to hinder progress.

To address these challenges, it is crucial to promote inclusivity, diversity, and equal opportunities for African Americans in all aspects of sports and entertainment. This requires ongoing commitment from stakeholders, including sports organizations, media outlets, and society as a whole.

By providing platforms and support for African American athletes and entertainers, we can ensure that their contributions and experiences are valued and celebrated. This will not only foster greater representation but also enrich the broader cultural landscape, promoting understanding and unity.

In conclusion, African American athletes and entertainers have had a profound influence on sports and popular culture. Their extraordinary achievements, resilience, and trailblazing spirit have shattered barriers and inspired generations. By recognizing and celebrating the African American influence in sports and pop culture, we can embrace a more inclusive and diverse society, promoting equality and social progress.

Chapter 5: Immigrant Contributions and Cultural Exchange

Section 1: Contributions of Asian Immigrants

Subsection 1: Impact of Chinese Immigrants on US History

The impact of Chinese immigrants on US history is a significant and often overlooked aspect of the country's cultural development. From the mid-19th century onwards, Chinese immigrants played a vital role in shaping various industries, influencing American society, and contributing to the nation's economic growth. This section highlights the key contributions of Chinese immigrants in several areas, including infrastructure, mining, agriculture, and cuisine.

Railroad Construction and Infrastructure

One of the most notable contributions of Chinese immigrants to US history was their involvement in the construction of the Transcontinental Railroad. Chinese laborers formed the majority of the workforce, particularly in the western part of the project. Their tireless efforts in laying tracks, blasting tunnels, and overcoming challenging terrain were instrumental in connecting the East and West coasts of the United States. The completion of the railroad in 1869 not only revolutionized transportation but also facilitated the expansion of trade and commerce across the country.

Mining and Gold Rush

Chinese immigrants played a crucial role in the famous California Gold Rush of the mid-19th century. They actively participated in mining operations, searching for gold in rivers and streams and working in the mines. Their expertise in gold mining techniques, such as hydraulic mining, significantly contributed to the success of mining operations. Chinese miners developed innovative sluice boxes and high-pressure water cannons, which greatly increased the efficiency and productivity of gold extraction. Moreover, they formed vibrant Chinese communities in mining towns, contributing to the multicultural fabric of early Californian society.

Agriculture and Food Culture

Chinese immigrants made significant contributions to the agricultural industry in the United States. They introduced and popularized various crops, including rice, tea, and a variety of fruits and vegetables. Chinese immigrants played a crucial role in developing advanced farming techniques and irrigation methods, making agriculture more efficient and productive.

Chinese cuisine also had a profound influence on American food culture. The introduction of dishes like chop suey, dim sum, and fortune cookies introduced Americans to a new world of flavors and culinary traditions. Chinese restaurants and food establishments became a vibrant part of American cities, offering diverse dining experiences.

Challenges and Discrimination

While Chinese immigrants made numerous contributions to US history, they also faced significant challenges and discrimination. The Chinese Exclusion Act of 1882, for example, severely restricted Chinese immigration and imposed harsh conditions on Chinese residents. Chinese immigrants often endured prejudice, racism, and segregated living conditions.

Despite facing adversities, Chinese immigrants persevered, establishing strong communities and making lasting contributions to the fabric of American society. Their resilience and determination paved the way for future generations to thrive and excel in various fields.

Cultural Heritage and Modern Influence

The impact of Chinese immigrants on US history extends beyond the industries they helped shape. Their cultural heritage, traditions, and values continue to enrich American society today. Chinese festivals such as the Lunar New Year and the Dragon Boat Festival have become widely celebrated across the country. Traditional Chinese martial arts, calligraphy, and other cultural practices have also gained popularity and influence.

Furthermore, Chinese-American individuals have excelled in various professions, including academia, science, technology, arts, and literature. Their achievements demonstrate the influence and contributions of Chinese immigrants to the cultural and intellectual landscape of the United States.

Conclusion

The impact of Chinese immigrants on US history is undeniable. Their contributions in railroad construction, mining, agriculture, and cuisine have left a lasting legacy. Despite facing discrimination and challenges, their resilience and determination have shaped American society and culture. By recognizing and celebrating the impact of Chinese immigrants, we honor their place in US history and acknowledge the importance of diversity and inclusion in our collective narrative.

Subsection 2: Japanese American Achievements and Cultural Influence

Japanese Americans have made significant contributions to various fields, including art, technology, business, and politics. Their achievements and cultural influence have played a vital role in shaping the cultural landscape of America. In this subsection, we will explore some of the notable achievements and contributions of Japanese Americans and how their cultural heritage has influenced American society.

Art and Design

Japanese Americans have made substantial contributions to the field of art and design, influencing both traditional and contemporary art movements. One well-known Japanese American artist is Isamu Noguchi, who is celebrated for his sculptures, gardens, and furniture designs. Noguchi's work blends Western modernism with traditional Japanese aesthetics, creating a unique fusion of cultures.

Another notable figure is Ruth Asawa, a Japanese American sculptor known for her intricate wire sculptures. Asawa's work expands the boundaries of sculpture and challenges conventional artistic techniques. Her innovative use of wire as a sculptural medium has inspired countless artists and continues to impact the art world today.

Technological Advancements

Japanese Americans have made significant contributions to technology and innovation. One prominent example is Jerry Yang, co-founder of Yahoo!, one of the earliest and most influential internet companies. Yang's entrepreneurial spirit and technological expertise have shaped the digital landscape, revolutionizing how people access information and connect with each other.

In addition to the tech industry, Japanese Americans have played a crucial role in advancements in robotics and engineering. Takeo Kanade, a Japanese American computer scientist, is renowned for his groundbreaking work in computer vision and robotics. Kanade's research and inventions have had a profound impact on fields such as autonomous vehicles, medical imaging, and augmented reality.

Business and Entrepreneurship

Japanese Americans have excelled in the world of business and entrepreneurship, leaving an indelible mark on the American economy. One notable figure is Daniel K. Inouye, who became the first Japanese American elected to the United States Senate. Inouye's political career was characterized by his advocacy for small businesses and economic development, making him a prominent leader in the Japanese American community.

Moreover, Japanese Americans have established successful businesses across various industries, showcasing their entrepreneurial skills and cultural influence. The contributions of Japanese American-owned businesses can be seen in sectors such as food, retail, and entertainment. From sushi restaurants to martial arts studios, these businesses have not only become staples in American communities but also promoted cultural exchange and understanding.

Cultural Preservation and Education

Japanese American cultural heritage has been preserved and promoted through various educational and cultural institutions. The Japanese American National

Museum, located in Los Angeles, serves as a vital resource for preserving and exhibiting Japanese American history, art, and culture. Through educational programs and exhibits, the museum fosters a deeper understanding and appreciation of Japanese American contributions.

Japanese American internment during World War II brought tremendous challenges and hardships, yet the resilience of the community led to the establishment of numerous cultural organizations. These organizations, such as community centers and heritage schools, focus on preserving and passing on Japanese language, arts, and traditions to future generations. By doing so, they ensure that Japanese American culture and heritage continue to thrive in the United States.

Japanese American Redress and Reconciliation

Japanese Americans have also played a significant role in advocating for redress and reconciliation regarding their internment during World War II. The Civil Liberties Act of 1988, signed into law by President Ronald Reagan, acknowledged and apologized for the unjust internment of Japanese Americans. This legislative victory was largely a result of the tireless efforts of Japanese American activists and community leaders.

The redress movement sought not only acknowledgment and financial restitution but also aimed to raise awareness about the importance of civil rights and the need to defend the rights of all Americans. The resilience and determination of Japanese Americans in seeking justice have served as a powerful reminder of the importance of protecting civil liberties and standing up against discrimination.

Overall, Japanese Americans have made significant achievements and contributions across various fields, enriching American society with their unique cultural heritage. Their artistic expressions, technological innovations, entrepreneurial endeavors, cultural preservation efforts, and advocacy for justice have had a lasting impact on American culture and serve as a testament to the power of diversity and inclusion.

Resources: - Japanese American National Museum: `https://www.janm.org/` - Isamu Noguchi Foundation and Garden Museum: `https://www.noguchi.org/` - Ruth Asawa: `https://ruthasawa.com/` - Jerry Yang: `https://www.jerryyang.com/` - Takeo Kanade: `https://ncar.xyz/iam597/computer-architecture-2/deep-takeo-kanade` - Daniel K. Inouye Institute: `https://www.inouyeinstitute.org/` - Civil Liberties Act of 1988:

https://www.congress.gov/bill/100th-congress/house-bill/442
- Japanese American Citizens League: https://jacl.org/

Exercises:

1. Research the life and work of one Japanese American artist and write a short essay about their artistic contributions and cultural influence.

2. Explore the history of Japanese American internment during World War II and discuss the long-term impact of the redress movement on civil rights in the United States.

3. Visit a local Japanese American cultural organization or museum and write a reflection on how their exhibits and programs promote cultural understanding.

4. Imagine you are a Japanese American entrepreneur starting a business. Develop a business plan that incorporates elements of Japanese culture and explains how you would foster cultural exchange within your community.

5. Investigate the recent advancements in robotics and computer vision and discuss the role of Japanese Americans in these fields. Highlight specific individuals or projects that have made significant contributions.

Remember to cite your sources and provide references for any research conducted during the completion of these exercises.

Caveats:

It is essential to approach the topic of Japanese American achievements and cultural influence with sensitivity and respect. The internment of Japanese Americans during World War II was a dark period in American history, and it is crucial to acknowledge the injustices they faced while also celebrating their triumphs. Additionally, while this subsection focuses on Japanese Americans, it is essential to recognize that Japanese culture extends beyond this specific community and encompasses diverse experiences and contributions.

Subsection 3: South Asian Contributions to Science and Technology

South Asia is a region rich in scientific and technological advancements that have shaped our understanding of the world. In this section, we will explore some of the significant contributions made by South Asian scientists and thinkers in various fields.

Ancient Indian Mathematics

One of the most remarkable achievements of South Asian scientists is the development of ancient Indian mathematics. The concept of zero, decimal system, and place value were first introduced in Indian mathematics. The famous mathematician Aryabhata from the 5th century made significant contributions to trigonometry, algebra, and number theory.

Let's take a look at a problem that showcases the brilliance of ancient Indian mathematicians:

Problem 1: Solve the quadratic equation $x^2 + 5x + 6 = 0$.

Solution: In order to solve the quadratic equation, we can apply the quadratic formula derived by ancient Indian mathematicians:

$$x = \frac{-b \pm \sqrt{b^2 - 4ac}}{2a}$$

In our case, $a = 1$, $b = 5$, and $c = 6$. Plugging these values into the formula, we get:

$$x = \frac{-5 \pm \sqrt{5^2 - 4 \cdot 1 \cdot 6}}{2 \cdot 1}$$

Simplifying further, we have:

$$x = \frac{-5 \pm \sqrt{1}}{2}$$

So, the solutions to the quadratic equation are $x_1 = -3$ and $x_2 = -2$.

Astronomy and Astrology

South Asia has a long history of advancements in both astronomy and astrology. Ancient astronomers from this region made significant contributions to our understanding of celestial bodies and the movements of planets.

One of the most famous instances is the discovery of the precession of the equinoxes by Indian astronomer Aryabhata. This discovery has far-reaching implications in the field of celestial mechanics.

In addition to astronomy, astrology has been an important part of South Asian culture for centuries. Even though astrology is not considered a science in modern times, it has played a vital role in shaping the beliefs and traditions of the region.

Medical Science and Ayurveda

Another major contribution of South Asia is the development of medical science, particularly Ayurveda. Ayurveda is an ancient system of medicine that has been practiced in the region for thousands of years.

Ayurvedic principles are based on a holistic approach to health, focusing on balance and harmony between the mind, body, and spirit. It encompasses various practices, including herbal medicine, dietary guidelines, and yoga.

Problem 2: Applying Ayurvedic Principles for Digestive Health

Ayurveda emphasizes the importance of maintaining a healthy digestive system for overall well-being. Let's consider the following problem:

Jane has been experiencing frequent digestive issues such as bloating and gas. She wants to incorporate Ayurvedic principles into her lifestyle to improve her digestive health. What dietary and lifestyle changes should Jane make?

Solution: According to Ayurveda, Jane can make the following dietary and lifestyle changes:

1. Eat a balanced diet: Include a variety of whole grains, fruits, vegetables, lean proteins, and healthy fats in your meals. Avoid processed and fried foods.
2. Practice mindful eating: Eat slowly and chew your food thoroughly. Avoid distractions while eating, such as watching TV or using electronic devices.
3. Include digestive spices: Incorporate spices like cumin, coriander, fennel, and ginger into your meals. These spices help improve digestion.
4. Drink warm water: Sip warm water throughout the day to stimulate digestion and reduce bloating.
5. Practice stress management: Stress can negatively impact digestion. Engage in relaxation techniques like deep breathing, meditation, or yoga to manage stress levels.

Implementing these changes can help Jane improve her digestive health and overall well-being.

Technology Innovations

South Asia has also played a significant role in technological advancements. The region is known for its contributions to computer science, information technology, and telecommunications.

One notable example is the invention of the "zero" and the decimal numeral system mentioned earlier. These concepts paved the way for the development of modern computing and algorithms.

In recent years, South Asian scientists and entrepreneurs have made significant contributions to the fields of artificial intelligence, data science, and software engineering. Their breakthroughs have had a profound impact on various industries worldwide.

Problem 3: Artificial Intelligence in South Asia

Artificial intelligence (AI) is a rapidly growing field that has the potential to revolutionize various sectors. How has South Asia contributed to the development and application of AI?

Solution: South Asia has made significant contributions to the field of AI. Researchers from the region have developed innovative AI algorithms and models that have advanced the state of the art. They have also played a crucial role in applying AI to sectors such as healthcare, agriculture, finance, and transportation.

One example of South Asian AI innovation is the development of speech recognition technologies for regional languages in India. This breakthrough enables more effective communication and accessibility for non-English speakers.

Furthermore, South Asian start-ups have been at the forefront of developing AI-enabled solutions for poverty alleviation, disaster management, and improving the quality of education.

The contributions of South Asia to science and technology are vast and diverse. From ancient mathematics and astronomy to modern-day technological innovations, the intellectual wealth of the region has shaped our world in numerous ways. It is crucial to recognize and appreciate the contributions made by South Asian scientists and thinkers to foster a more inclusive and comprehensive understanding of the history of science and technology.

Subsection 4: Influence of Southeast Asian Refugees on American Art

Southeast Asian refugees have made significant contributions to American art, enriching the cultural landscape and influencing various art forms. In this subsection, we will explore the profound impact of Southeast Asian refugees on American art, highlighting their unique perspectives, artistic expressions, and the challenges they have faced.

Background

The influx of Southeast Asian refugees into the United States occurred primarily in the aftermath of the Vietnam War and the Khmer Rouge regime in Cambodia. These refugees brought with them a rich cultural heritage and artistic traditions, seeking new opportunities and a safe haven in the United States. Overcoming the trauma and hardships they experienced, Southeast Asian refugees found solace and expression through their art, contributing to the vibrant diversity of American art.

Artistic Themes and Styles

Southeast Asian refugees have expressed their experiences, emotions, and cultural identities through various artistic themes and styles. Their artwork reflects a fusion of traditional Southeast Asian aesthetics with contemporary American influences, creating a distinctive visual language that resonates with both Southeast Asian and American audiences.

One prevalent theme explored by Southeast Asian refugee artists is the notion of displacement and the search for identity. Their artwork often depicts the sense of longing for their homeland, the difficulties of adapting to a new culture, and the complexities of navigating a dual identity. These themes are beautifully captured in paintings, sculptures, and mixed-media installations, exhibiting a blend of traditional Southeast Asian motifs and modern artistic techniques.

Moreover, Southeast Asian refugee artists have also drawn inspiration from the natural environment, using art to convey their deep connection to nature and the healing power it provides. Through vibrant landscapes, intricate botanical illustrations, and delicate sculptures, they celebrate the beauty of their homelands while also embracing their new surroundings in the United States.

Challenges and Resilience

The journey of Southeast Asian refugees to establish themselves in the American art scene has not been without challenges. Overcoming language barriers, financial constraints, and cultural differences, they have demonstrated remarkable resilience and determination to share their stories and artistic expressions.

One significant challenge faced by Southeast Asian refugee artists is the lack of representation and visibility in mainstream art institutions. Historically, the art world has been dominated by Eurocentric perspectives, often overlooking the contributions of artists from diverse backgrounds. As a result, Southeast Asian refugee artists have had to navigate alternative art spaces, community organizations, and grassroots movements to showcase their work and connect with audiences who appreciate their unique cultural perspectives.

Despite these challenges, Southeast Asian refugee artists have found strength in their communities and have formed networks of support and collaboration. They have utilized their collective voices to advocate for greater representation and inclusion in the art world, working towards dismantling barriers and creating space for their artistic expressions.

Examples of Southeast Asian Refugee Artists

To appreciate the diversity and impact of Southeast Asian refugee artists on American art, let us explore the works of two influential individuals:

Dinh Q. Lê is a Vietnamese-American artist known for his thought-provoking photographic and installation works. Lê's oeuvre often reflects his experiences as a Vietnamese refugee, exploring themes of memory, identity, and post-war trauma. Through his captivating use of fragmented imagery and storytelling techniques, Lê challenges viewers to confront the complexities of history and the lasting impact of war.

Leang Seckon is a Cambodian-American artist celebrated for his vibrant mixed-media artworks that blend traditional Cambodian artistic forms with contemporary expressions. Seckon's paintings depict scenes from Cambodian history, folklore, and daily life, encapsulating the resilience and beauty of his homeland. Through his art, he aims to preserve Cambodian cultural heritage and convey the experiences of Cambodian refugees.

Further Exploration

To explore the influence of Southeast Asian refugees on American art further, consider visiting local art galleries, museums, and cultural organizations that prioritize exhibiting the works of diverse artists. Engage in conversations with Southeast Asian refugee artists and attend artist talks or panel discussions to gain a deeper understanding of their experiences and artistic practices. Additionally, exploring art criticism, scholarly articles, and documentaries focused on Southeast Asian American art can provide valuable insights into this rich and often underrepresented artistic tradition.

Conclusion

The influence of Southeast Asian refugees on American art is undeniable. Their unique perspectives, artistic expressions, and resilience continue to shape and enrich the contemporary art scene. By recognizing and celebrating their contributions, we not only embrace the diversity of American art but also acknowledge the transformative power of art in exploring complex narratives and fostering cultural understanding. So let us appreciate and honor the profound impact of Southeast Asian refugee artists on American art.

Subsection 5: Filipino American Influence in the Labor Movement

Filipino Americans have made significant contributions to the labor movement in the United States. This subsection will explore the history of their involvement, their impact on worker's rights, and their struggles for fair treatment in the workplace.

Historical Background

Filipino migration to the United States began in the early 20th century, driven by economic opportunities and the demand for labor in industries such as agriculture, fishing, and domestic work. Many Filipinos found employment in farms, plantations, and canneries, often facing exploitative working conditions and low wages.

Organizing Efforts

Filipino immigrants faced discrimination and racism, which motivated them to join labor unions and fight for their rights. One notable organization was the Filipino Agricultural Laborers Association (FALA), founded in 1933, which aimed to empower Filipino farmworkers and address their grievances.

Another important figure in the labor movement was Philip Vera Cruz, a Filipino American farmworker who co-founded the Agricultural Workers Organizing Committee (AWOC) in the 1950s. AWOC played a crucial role in the Delano Grape Strike of 1965, a landmark event in the history of the labor movement, which eventually led to the formation of the United Farm Workers (UFW) union.

The Delano Grape Strike

The Delano Grape Strike was a pivotal moment in Filipino American labor history. Filipino farmworkers, led by figures like Larry Itliong and Philip Vera Cruz, joined forces with Mexican American workers, led by Cesar Chavez, to protest against poor working conditions and low wages in the grape industry.

The strike, which lasted for five years, garnered national attention and support from various civil rights activists and organizations. Filipino American workers played a crucial role in organizing and sustaining the strike, demonstrating their commitment to fighting for better working conditions, wages, and dignity.

Legacy and Impact

The Filipino American labor movement left a lasting impact on the overall labor movement in the United States. The Delano Grape Strike showed the power of solidarity in achieving social and economic justice for agricultural workers. It also paved the way for the broader recognition of the rights of all farmworkers, regardless of their ethnic backgrounds.

Filipino Americans' involvement in the labor movement challenged stereotypes and discrimination, while also highlighting the vital role they played in building communities and contributing to the progress of the nation. Their resilience and determination inspire future generations to continue advocating for fair treatment in the workplace.

Contemporary Challenges

Despite the successes and contributions of Filipino American workers in the labor movement, challenges persist. Many continue to face issues such as wage theft, unsafe working conditions, and limited access to healthcare and benefits. Language barriers and cultural differences also pose additional hurdles.

To address these challenges, organizations like the Filipino Worker Center (FWC) and the National Alliance for Filipino Concerns (NAFCON) provide resources, support, and advocacy for Filipino American workers. These groups work towards promoting fair labor practices, educating workers about their rights, and fostering community solidarity.

Conclusion

The Filipino American influence in the labor movement cannot be overstated. Their contributions have advanced the cause of workers' rights and highlighted the importance of unity across ethnicities in the pursuit of justice. By understanding and appreciating the history of Filipino American labor activism, we can work towards creating a more equitable and inclusive society for all workers.

Section 2: European Immigration and Cultural Impact

Subsection 1: Italian and Irish American Contributions

Italian and Irish Americans have made significant contributions to various aspects of American society, including politics, labor movements, arts, and sports. This subsection explores some of their remarkable accomplishments and the impact they have had on American culture.

Political Contributions

Italian and Irish Americans have played crucial roles in shaping American politics. They have served in various government positions and have made significant contributions at local, state, and national levels. For example, Fiorello La Guardia, an Italian American, served as the mayor of New York City from 1934 to 1945. La Guardia's reforms and policies transformed the city and contributed to its growth and development. His innovative ideas set new standards for urban administration.

Similarly, the Irish American community has produced prominent political figures, including John F. Kennedy, who became the 35th President of the United States. Kennedy's presidency symbolized the advancement of Irish Americans in politics and inspired many to pursue leadership roles.

Labor Movements

Italian and Irish Americans have been influential in labor movements, fighting for workers' rights and fair treatment. They actively participated in trade unions and played key roles in advocating for better working conditions and higher wages. For instance, James R. Hoffa, an Irish American labor union leader, served as the president of the International Brotherhood of Teamsters. Under his leadership, the union grew significantly in membership and bargaining power, resulting in improved working conditions for many workers.

Italian Americans also made significant contributions to labor movements, particularly in industries such as mining and garment manufacturing. They fought for the rights of marginalized workers, advocating for fair wages, safe working conditions, and the abolition of child labor.

Arts and Literature

Italian and Irish Americans have left a lasting impact on American arts and literature. Italian American artists, such as Frank Stella and Carolee Schneemann, made significant contributions to contemporary art movements. Their works pushed boundaries and challenged traditional artistic conventions, influencing subsequent generations of artists.

Irish American writers, including James Joyce and William Butler Yeats, have produced literary masterpieces that continue to be celebrated globally. Their works explore themes of identity, culture, and the human condition, leaving a profound mark on the literary landscape.

Sports and Entertainment

Italian and Irish Americans have excelled in the world of sports and entertainment, showcasing their talent and becoming role models for aspiring athletes and performers. In sports, notable Italian American figures include Joe DiMaggio, a legendary baseball player, and Rocky Marciano, an undefeated heavyweight boxing champion.

Irish American contributions to sports are equally impressive, with notable figures such as Babe Ruth, one of the greatest baseball players of all time. Ruth's athletic prowess and charismatic personality made him an American icon.

In the entertainment industry, Italian and Irish Americans have made significant contributions through acting, music, and comedy. Celebrities like Robert De Niro, Al Pacino, and Bruce Springsteen have achieved fame and success, captivating audiences worldwide with their talent and creativity.

Cultural Heritage

Italian and Irish Americans have preserved their rich cultural heritage, celebrating their traditions through festivals, parades, and other social events. The annual St. Patrick's Day parades, celebrated by Irish Americans, have become a cherished tradition in many American cities. Similarly, Italian American heritage festivals, like the Feast of San Gennaro in New York City, showcase the vibrant Italian culture, featuring traditional food, music, and performances.

These cultural events not only allow Italian and Irish Americans to connect with their roots but also provide an opportunity for others to appreciate and learn about their heritage.

Contemporary Influence

Italian and Irish American contributions continue to influence contemporary American culture. Their impact can be seen in various fields, including food, fashion, and popular culture. Italian cuisine, with its diverse regional dishes, has become an integral part of American culinary traditions. Pizza, pasta, and gelato are just a few examples of the Italian culinary delights that have been embraced by Americans nationwide.

Irish American influence can be observed in the popularity of Irish pubs, where people gather to enjoy live music and traditional Irish fare. Irish music and dance, such as the iconic Irish step dancing, also continue to captivate audiences and inspire new generations of performers.

In conclusion, Italian and Irish Americans have made significant contributions to American society, leaving a lasting impact on politics, labor movements, arts, sports, and cultural heritage. Their achievements have enriched American culture and serve as a testament to the diversity and strength of the nation. It is important to recognize and appreciate the contributions of these communities to foster a more inclusive and comprehensive understanding of American history.

Subsection 2: Eastern European Influence on American Literature

The literary landscape of America has been greatly enriched by the contributions of writers from Eastern Europe. These authors bring with them unique perspectives, storytelling techniques, and cultural backgrounds that have had a lasting impact on American literature. In this subsection, we will explore the influence of Eastern European writers on various aspects of American literature, including themes, styles, and narrative structures.

Literary Themes

One of the significant contributions of Eastern European writers to American literature is the exploration of universal themes that resonate with readers across cultures. Many Eastern European authors have delved into themes of oppression, totalitarianism, exile, and the struggle for personal and political freedom. Their firsthand experiences with the turbulent history of Eastern Europe have informed their writing, allowing them to present these themes in a profound and thought-provoking manner.

An example of an Eastern European writer who has had a profound impact on American literature is Vladimir Nabokov. Born in Russia, Nabokov's works often explore themes of exile and displacement. His most famous novel, "Lolita," challenges societal norms and probes the depths of human desire. By introducing taboo subjects and examining the darker aspects of the human psyche, Nabokov's work has influenced a generation of American writers.

Narrative Styles

Eastern European writers have also introduced unique narrative styles to American literature. These writers often employ intricate storytelling techniques, nonlinear narratives, and unreliable narrators to create a sense of ambiguity and complexity in their works. These narrative techniques challenge readers to question traditional notions of reality and engage with the text on a deeper level.

One notable example of an Eastern European writer who has impacted American literature through innovative narrative styles is Milan Kundera. Kundera's novel "The Unbearable Lightness of Being" weaves together multiple storylines, philosophical musings, and historical events to create a rich tapestry of human experience. Kundera's experimentation with narrative structure has influenced American authors to push the boundaries of traditional storytelling and explore new ways of presenting their narratives.

Cultural Heritage

Eastern European writers have also played a crucial role in preserving and celebrating their cultural heritage through their works. By incorporating elements of folklore, mythology, and historical events from Eastern Europe, these writers have introduced readers to a rich and diverse cultural landscape.

A prime example of an Eastern European writer who has celebrated his cultural heritage in American literature is Isaac Bashevis Singer. Singer, a Polish-born Jewish writer, frequently draws upon Jewish folklore, traditions, and history in his stories. His works, such as "Gimpel the Fool" and "The Slave," provide a glimpse into the world of Eastern European Jews and serve as a powerful reminder of the importance of cultural heritage and identity.

Literature as a Form of Resistance

Eastern European writers have often used literature as a form of resistance against oppressive regimes and censorship. Through their words, these authors have challenged the status quo, exposed injustices, and advocated for social and political change.

A notable example of an Eastern European writer who utilized literature as a tool for resistance is Aleksandr Solzhenitsyn. Solzhenitsyn's novel "One Day in the Life of Ivan Denisovich" depicts life in a Soviet labor camp and exposes the harsh realities of the gulag system. By shining a light on the darker side of Soviet society, Solzhenitsyn's work contributed to a growing awareness of human rights abuses and became a catalyst for change.

In conclusion, the influence of Eastern European writers on American literature cannot be overstated. Their unique perspectives, narrative styles, and exploration of universal themes have shaped and enriched the literary landscape of America. Through their works, Eastern European authors have brought to the forefront important issues, challenged traditional storytelling techniques, and celebrated their cultural heritage. Their contributions serve as a testament to the power of literature to bridge cultural divides and inspire social change.

Subsection 3: German and Jewish American Achievements

German and Jewish immigrants have made significant contributions to American society in various fields, including science, arts, and philosophy. Their achievements have had a profound impact on American culture and have helped shape the country into what it is today. In this section, we will explore some of the notable accomplishments of German and Jewish Americans and their lasting legacies.

German Contributions to Science and Technology

German scientists and engineers have played a crucial role in advancing scientific knowledge and technological innovations in the United States. One notable example is Albert Einstein, a German-born physicist who revolutionized our understanding of the universe with his theory of relativity. Einstein's contributions to theoretical physics earned him the Nobel Prize in Physics in 1921.

Another prominent German scientist is Wernher von Braun, who immigrated to the United States after World War II. Von Braun was a key figure in the development of rocket technology and played a vital role in the space race between the United States and the Soviet Union. His work at NASA contributed to the successful moon landing in 1969.

In addition to these groundbreaking achievements, German Americans have also made significant contributions to various fields of science, including chemistry, biology, and medicine. For example, Fritz Haber, a German chemist, made groundbreaking discoveries in the field of chemical reactions and was awarded the Nobel Prize in Chemistry in 1918.

Jewish Contributions to Literature and Intellectual Movements

Jewish Americans have made a lasting impact on American literature and intellectual movements, enriching the country's cultural fabric. One notable figure is Franz Kafka, a Jewish writer born in Prague. Kafka's works, such as "The Metamorphosis" and "The Trial," explored themes of existentialism and the human condition, influencing generations of writers and thinkers.

Another influential Jewish American writer is Saul Bellow, who won the Nobel Prize in Literature in 1976. Bellow's novels, including "The Adventures of Augie

March" and "Herzog," captured the essence of American life and tackled themes of identity, immigration, and the search for meaning.

Jewish intellectuals have also played a pivotal role in shaping intellectual movements in America. The Frankfurt School, a group of German-Jewish philosophers and social theorists, had a profound impact on critical theory and cultural studies. Figures like Theodor Adorno and Herbert Marcuse brought perspectives on ideology, mass media, and capitalism that continue to shape academic discourse today.

German and Jewish Influence on Contemporary Culture

The influence of German and Jewish Americans extends beyond their individual achievements. Their impact can be seen in various aspects of contemporary culture, including film, music, and philosophy.

German Expressionist cinema, which emerged in the 1920s, has had a lasting impact on the art of filmmaking. Directors like Fritz Lang and F.W. Murnau introduced groundbreaking techniques and visual storytelling elements that continue to inspire filmmakers to this day. Lang's iconic film "Metropolis" and Murnau's masterpiece "Nosferatu" are considered timeless classics.

Jewish composers and musicians have also shaped the American music landscape. From Gershwin to Bernstein, Jewish American musicians have made significant contributions to classical, jazz, and popular music genres. Their compositions and performances have captivated audiences and enriched American cultural heritage.

Moreover, German and Jewish philosophers have contributed to the development of contemporary philosophy. Figures like Martin Heidegger, Hannah Arendt, and Emmanuel Levinas have explored profound questions about ethics, existence, and human nature. Their ideas have influenced philosophical discourse, challenging conventional wisdom and expanding our understanding of the world.

Cultural Exchange and Integration

The achievements of German and Jewish Americans reflect the ability of immigrant communities to enrich their adopted homeland through cultural exchange and integration. The blending of German and Jewish traditions with American culture has created a diverse and vibrant society.

Furthermore, the success of German and Jewish Americans can be attributed not only to their individual talents but also to the opportunities and freedoms offered by the United States. America's embrace of diverse cultures and its commitment to equal opportunity have allowed these communities to thrive and contribute to the overall progress of the nation.

Conclusion

German and Jewish immigrants have brought unique perspectives, talents, and contributions to the United States. Their achievements in science, arts, and philosophy have left an indelible mark on American culture. By recognizing and celebrating their accomplishments, we acknowledge the immense value of diversity and the profound impact that minority communities have had in shaping our collective history. As we continue to explore the contributions of other minority groups, we must strive to create a narrative of history that reflects the true mosaic of humanity.

Subsection 4: Scandinavian Cultural Contributions in the Midwest

Scandinavian cultural contributions have had a significant impact on the Midwest region of the United States. The presence of Scandinavian immigrants and their descendants in states like Minnesota, Wisconsin, North Dakota, and Iowa has created a rich cultural tapestry that is still celebrated today. From art and design to literature and food, the Scandinavian influence is deeply ingrained in the fabric of the Midwest.

Scandinavian Art and Design

Scandinavian art and design have left an indelible mark on the Midwest. With its clean lines, functional aesthetic, and emphasis on natural materials, Scandinavian design has been adopted and embraced by the region. Furniture, household items, and architecture in the Midwest often showcase the influence of Scandinavian design principles.

For example, the renowned architect Frank Lloyd Wright, who spent much of his career in the Midwest, was greatly influenced by Nordic design. The simplicity, harmony with nature, and focus on craftsmanship found in Scandinavian architecture resonated with Wright's own philosophy. Some of his most iconic designs, such as the Gammelgården Swedish Immigrant Museum in Minnesota, showcase the fusion of Scandinavian and Prairie School architectural styles.

Literature and Folklore

Scandinavian literature and folklore have also found a home in the Midwest. The stories of Norse mythology, with their epic tales of gods and heroes, have captured the imagination of many in the region. Scandinavian immigrants brought with them a rich oral and written tradition that has been passed down through generations.

One famous Scandinavian literary figure with ties to the Midwest is Norwegian-American author O.E. Rølvaag. His novel, "Giants in the Earth," depicts the struggles of Norwegian pioneers on the Midwest prairie and is considered a classic of American literature. Rølvaag's work not only portrays the challenges faced by immigrants but also highlights their resilience and determination.

Cuisine and Culinary Traditions

The culinary traditions of Scandinavia have also made their mark on the Midwest's food scene. The region is known for its Scandinavian-inspired dishes, such as Swedish meatballs, lutefisk, and lefse. Many small towns in the Midwest host annual Scandinavian festivals, where traditional foods and drinks are showcased and enjoyed by locals and visitors alike.

In recent years, there has been a resurgence of interest in Nordic cuisine, with a focus on using locally sourced ingredients and traditional cooking techniques. This farm-to-table approach aligns well with the Midwest's agricultural heritage, creating a unique fusion of Scandinavian and Midwest flavors.

Cultural Festivals and Traditions

Scandinavian cultural festivals and traditions play a vital role in preserving and celebrating heritage in the Midwest. These events bring together communities to showcase Scandinavian music, dance, crafts, and fashion. One prominent festival is the "Dala Horse Trot" in Lindsborg, Kansas, where participants parade through town with their handcrafted Dala horses, a symbol of Swedish culture.

In addition to festivals, many Scandinavian communities in the Midwest have established cultural centers, museums, and historical societies that aim to preserve and educate future generations about their heritage. These institutions serve as gathering places for the community and offer opportunities to learn about Scandinavian history, language, and customs.

Cross-Cultural Exchange

The influence of Scandinavian culture in the Midwest is not limited to the Scandinavian-American community. The unique blend of Scandinavian and Midwest traditions has led to cross-cultural exchange and the integration of Scandinavian elements into mainstream Midwestern culture.

For example, the Danish concept of "hygge," which denotes coziness, comfort, and a feeling of well-being, has gained popularity beyond the Scandinavian community. The idea of creating warm and inviting spaces, enjoying good company, and embracing simple pleasures has resonated with people from all walks of life in the Midwest.

Additionally, the Scandinavian focus on environmental sustainability and social welfare has also influenced the Midwest's approach to these issues. Many communities in the region have embraced renewable energy sources, implemented sustainable farming practices, and fostered a sense of community involvement and support.

In conclusion, Scandinavian cultural contributions in the Midwest have had a profound and lasting impact on the region. Through art, literature, cuisine, festivals, and cross-cultural exchange, the Scandinavian influence has become an integral part of the Midwest's identity. As time goes on, it is crucial to continue celebrating and honoring these contributions, ensuring that future generations appreciate the rich and diverse heritage that shapes their communities.

Subsection 5: Slavic American Traditions and Artistic Influence

Slavic American communities have made significant contributions to American culture, particularly in the realms of art, music, literature, and dance. The rich heritage brought by Slavic immigrants has left a lasting impact on American society, blending traditional Slavic artistic traditions with contemporary American influences. In this subsection, we will explore the unique traditions and artistic influence of Slavic Americans, highlighting their creative expressions and cultural contributions.

Slavic Visual Arts

Slavic American visual artists have played a vital role in shaping the American art scene. The works of Slavic American painters often incorporate elements of traditional Slavic aesthetics, while also reflecting the artist's personal experiences and cultural background. One notable artist is Vladimir Kush, a Ukrainian-born painter who now resides in the United States. Through his surrealist style, Kush merges Slavic symbolism with modern artistic techniques, creating intricate and thought-provoking masterpieces. Moreover, Slavic American sculptors like Chakaia Booker and Gyuri Hollosy have challenged traditional artistic norms, redefining sculpture with their innovative use of materials and cultural motifs.

Slavic Literary Contributions

Slavic American writers have crafted captivating narratives that explore themes of identity, immigration, and the human experience. Their works shed light on the challenges and triumphs of Slavic immigrants, offering unique perspectives on the American dream. For instance, the Pulitzer Prize-winning author Jhumpa Lahiri, born to Bengali parents in London and raised in Rhode Island, weaves captivating stories that reflect the struggles and joys of the immigrant experience. Similarly, Aleksandar Hemon, a Bosnian-American writer, delves into themes of displacement, war, and memory through his powerful novels and essays.

Slavic Dance and Music

Slavic American communities have upheld their cultural heritage through vibrant dance and music traditions. Folk dances like the Polish polka, Ukrainian hopak, and Russian troika have become integral parts of Slavic American celebrations and cultural events. These lively dances involve intricate footwork, colorful costumes, and energetic rhythms that showcase the joy and vitality of Slavic culture. Additionally, Slavic American musicians have made significant contributions to American music, fusing traditional Slavic melodies with modern genres. Grammy Award-winning polka musician Jimmy Sturr and renowned violinist Regina Carter are just a few examples of Slavic American artists who have left an indelible mark on the American music scene.

Preserving Slavic Traditions

Despite the challenges of assimilation and the passage of time, Slavic American communities remain dedicated to preserving their cultural heritage. Various organizations, such as folk dance groups, language schools, and cultural festivals, actively promote Slavic traditions among younger generations. These efforts ensure that Slavic artistic expressions and cultural practices continue to thrive in the United States. Moreover, digital platforms and social media have provided avenues for Slavic American artists to connect with wider audiences, showcasing their talent and traditions to the world.

Unconventional Example: The Slavic Street Art Movement

While street art may not be commonly associated with Slavic culture, a growing movement of Slavic American street artists has emerged, bringing their unique perspectives to the urban landscape. Influenced by the vibrant street art scenes in their ancestral countries and the diverse American street art culture, these artists infuse their works with Slavic symbolism and motifs. By blending traditional and contemporary elements, Slavic American street art challenges societal norms, provokes thought, and celebrates the cultural heritage of Slavic communities.

In conclusion, Slavic American traditions and artistic influence play a significant role in shaping American culture. Visual arts, literature, dance, and music are channels through which Slavic Americans express their unique identities and contributions. By melding traditional Slavic elements with contemporary American influences, Slavic American artists continue to enrich the cultural fabric of the United States.

Chapter 6: The Impact of Hispanic/Latinx Communities

Section 1: Pre-Columbian Civilizations and Contributions

Subsection 1: Mesoamerican Art and Architecture

Introduction

Mesoamerican art and architecture represent the rich cultural heritage of the indigenous civilizations that thrived in the region for thousands of years. From intricate sculptures to monumental structures, Mesoamerican art and architecture showcase the innovative techniques and profound beliefs of ancient civilizations such as the Maya, Aztec, and Olmec. In this section, we will explore the key elements, styles, and symbolic meanings behind Mesoamerican art and architecture, shedding light on their significance in understanding the cultural and historical context of the time.

Characteristics of Mesoamerican Art

Mesoamerican art is characterized by its intricate designs, bold colors, and a deep connection to nature and spirituality. The art forms encompass a wide range of mediums, including stone carving, pottery, mural painting, textiles, and precious metalwork. Here, we will delve into the distinctive features of Mesoamerican art.

1. Iconography and Symbolism Mesoamerican art is highly symbolic, often using intricate iconography to convey religious beliefs, mythological narratives, and social status. Symbols such as deities, animals, plants, and celestial bodies were utilized to represent various concepts and serve as a visual language for communication.

2. **Naturalistic and Abstract Styles** Mesoamerican art exhibits a blend of naturalistic and abstract styles. While some sculptures and murals portray human and animal figures in a realistic manner, others are stylized and abstract, emphasizing geometric shapes and patterns. This artistic diversity reflects the different artistic traditions within the Mesoamerican region.

3. **Hieroglyphic Writing** Mesoamerican art often incorporates hieroglyphic writing, a system of symbolic writing used by civilizations such as the Maya and Aztec. These intricate scripts were employed to record historical events, religious rituals, and astronomical knowledge. The combination of hieroglyphic writing and visual art creates a comprehensive narrative of Mesoamerican civilization.

Architectural Marvels of Mesoamerica

Mesoamerican architecture is renowned for its grandeur, precision, and alignment with cosmic principles. The impressive pyramids, temples, and palaces constructed by ancient civilizations continue to inspire awe and admiration. Let's explore the main characteristics and types of Mesoamerican architecture.

1. **Pyramids and Temples** Pyramids and temples were the backbone of Mesoamerican architectural achievements. These towering structures served as religious centers, dedicated to the worship of deities or as burial sites for revered rulers. The architecture incorporated precise alignments with astronomical phenomena, reflecting the Mesoamerican people's deep understanding of celestial bodies.

2. **Ball Courts** Ball courts were an integral part of Mesoamerican society, serving both recreational and ritual purposes. These elliptical or rectangular-shaped courts witnessed the ceremonial ball game known as "tlachtli" or "pok-a-tok." The architecture of the ball courts combined practical design with sacred symbolism, showcasing the civilizations' commitment to sports and religious beliefs.

3. **Palaces and Residential Structures** Palaces and residential structures were designed for the ruling elite and served as symbols of power and authority. The architecture of palaces often featured intricate carvings, expansive courtyards, and sophisticated drainage systems. These structures provided insight into the daily lives and social hierarchy of Mesoamerican societies.

Significance and Legacy

Mesoamerican art and architecture have significant cultural and historical importance. They provide a window into the beliefs, customs, and achievements of ancient civilizations, giving us valuable insights into their way of life. Additionally, the enduring legacy of Mesoamerican art can be seen in contemporary Mexican and Central American cultures, where traditional motifs and techniques continue to inspire modern artists and architects.

Summary

Mesoamerican art and architecture encompass a diverse array of artistic styles and architectural marvels. The symbolic iconography, intricate designs, and profound meanings embedded in these art forms offer a glimpse into the rich cultural heritage of ancient civilizations. From the grand pyramids to the intricate murals, Mesoamerican art and architecture leave an indelible mark on our understanding of history, cultural identity, and artistic expression.

Key Takeaways

- Mesoamerican art is characterized by intricate designs, bold colors, and a deep connection to nature and spirituality.
- Iconography, symbolism, and hieroglyphic writing play a significant role in conveying narratives and beliefs in Mesoamerican art.
- Mesoamerican architecture showcases grand pyramids, temples, ball courts, and palaces, demonstrating the civilizations' advanced engineering and alignment with cosmic principles.
- Mesoamerican art and architecture offer valuable insights into the cultural, historical, and artistic achievements of ancient civilizations, leaving a lasting legacy in contemporary cultures.

Now that we have explored the fascinating world of Mesoamerican art and architecture, let's move on to the next section of this chapter, where we will examine the contributions of Latinx artists to visual culture in the United States.

Subsection 2: Mayan and Aztec Scientific Advancements

The Mayan and Aztec civilizations, which flourished in Mesoamerica from around 2000 BCE to 1521 CE, made significant contributions to scientific knowledge.

These ancient cultures developed sophisticated systems for mathematics, astronomy, and medicine, which advanced their understanding of the natural world.

Mathematics

The Mayans and Aztecs developed highly advanced mathematical systems that allowed them to perform complex calculations and understand numerical relationships. One of their most notable achievements was the invention of zero as a placeholder in their number system. This concept of zero was a groundbreaking development in mathematics and had a profound impact on the field.

The Mayans and Aztecs also used base-20 number systems, as opposed to the base-10 system commonly used today. This system facilitated calculations involving large numbers and provided a more efficient means of record-keeping. They were able to perform addition, subtraction, multiplication, and division using their numerical notation.

In addition, the Mayans developed a precise calendar system known as the Long Count. This calendar incorporated cycles of various lengths, including the 260-day Tzolk'in and the 365-day Haab. These calendars allowed the Mayans to accurately track time and plan activities such as agricultural activities and religious ceremonies.

Astronomy

Both the Mayans and Aztecs were skilled astronomers and made significant advancements in understanding celestial bodies. They carefully observed the movements of the sun, moon, planets, and stars, and developed sophisticated astronomical calendars.

The Mayans, in particular, had a deep understanding of celestial cycles and were able to accurately predict astronomical events such as eclipses. They built observatories and used specialized instruments to observe and record celestial phenomena. Their knowledge of astronomy influenced their religious and agricultural practices, as well as their architecture and urban planning.

The Aztecs also had a keen interest in astronomy and incorporated celestial observations into their religious rituals and calendar systems. They constructed magnificent temples dedicated to celestial deities and developed a calendar based on the movements of the sun. Their calendar, known as the Tonalpohualli, consisted of a 260-day cycle that served as the foundation for their religious and cultural activities.

Medicine

The Mayans and Aztecs had a sophisticated understanding of medicine and developed effective treatments for a wide range of ailments. They relied on extensive knowledge of herbal medicine and used plants and natural substances to treat various illnesses and injuries.

Both civilizations had an impressive pharmacopoeia, containing remedies for fevers, infections, digestive disorders, and other ailments. Herbal remedies were often combined with spiritual rituals and ceremonies to enhance their healing properties.

The Mayans also had a deep understanding of human anatomy and performed surgical procedures, such as trepanation (drilling holes in the skull), for therapeutic and ritualistic purposes. They used plant-based anesthetics and had specialized tools for surgery.

The Aztecs practiced a form of medicine known as Nahuatl, which combined herbal remedies, spiritual healing, and physical therapies. They believed that illness was caused by imbalances in the body and used techniques such as bloodletting and purging to restore harmony.

Example Problem: The Mayan Calendar

Let's explore a problem related to the Mayan calendar system. The Mayan Long Count calendar uses a base-20 numbering system and consists of various cycles. One of the cycles is the baktun, which is equivalent to 144,000 days. A day in the Long Count calendar is represented as a combination of five different units: the k'in (1 day), the winal (20 days), the tun (360 days), the k'atun (7,200 days), and the baktun (144,000 days).

Suppose we want to convert a date in the Long Count calendar to the equivalent number of days. Let's say we have the following date: 9.18.0.0.0 (9 baktuns, 18 k'atuns, 0 tuns, 0 winals, and 0 k'ins).

To determine the number of days, we can multiply each unit by its corresponding value and sum them up. Using the given date, we would calculate:

$$\& = (9 \times 144,000) + (18 \times 7,200) + (0 \times 360) + (0 \times 20) + (0 \times 1)$$
$$\& = 1,296,000 + 129,600 + 0 + 0 + 0$$
$$\& = 1,425,600 \text{ days}$$

Therefore, the date 9.18.0.0.0 in the Mayan Long Count calendar corresponds to 1,425,600 days.

This problem illustrates how the Mayans' base-20 numbering system and the concept of cycles allowed them to track and record dates accurately.

Resources

To further explore the scientific achievements of the Mayans and Aztecs, here are some recommended resources:

- Book: "Maya Cosmos: Three Thousand Years on the Shaman's Path" by David Freidel, Linda Schele, and Joy Parker
- Documentary: "Lost Worlds: The Maya" (National Geographic)
- Website: "Maya Civilization" - National Geographic Society

These resources provide in-depth information about the Mayan and Aztec civilizations and their contributions to mathematics, astronomy, and medicine.

Conclusion

The Mayans and Aztecs were pioneering civilizations in the fields of mathematics, astronomy, and medicine. Their advancements in these areas not only influenced their own cultures but also left a lasting impact on scientific knowledge. The Mayan and Aztec achievements demonstrate the significant contributions of indigenous communities to the field of science and remind us of the diverse mosaic of human history.

Subsection 3: Contributions to Astronomy and Mathematics

Astronomy and mathematics are two interconnected disciplines that have played a crucial role in human understanding of the universe. Throughout history, various cultures, including indigenous peoples, have made significant contributions to both fields. In this section, we will explore some of the major contributions made by minority communities in the realms of astronomy and mathematics.

Ancient Knowledge Systems

Indigenous cultures around the world have developed sophisticated astronomical and mathematical knowledge systems. These systems are often intertwined with spiritual beliefs, cultural practices, and celestial observations. For example, the Mayans, an ancient Mesoamerican civilization, had precise astronomical calendars that allowed them to predict solar and lunar eclipses. They also developed a numerical system based on the concept of zero, which is a fundamental idea in mathematics today.

Mathematics in African Civilizations

African civilizations, such as the ancient Egyptians, have made significant contributions to mathematics. The Egyptians used a decimal numerical system, hieroglyphic symbols, and sophisticated geometrical techniques. They were adept in solving practical mathematical problems, such as calculating areas and volumes for architectural purposes. Moreover, they developed a rudimentary understanding of fractions and used them in their daily lives.

Indigenous Star Knowledge

Indigenous cultures have deep connections with the stars and have developed intricate knowledge systems to navigate, track time, and understand celestial events. The Polynesians, for example, were master navigators who used stars, planets, and currents to navigate vast oceans. They developed star compasses to aid their journeys and could accurately predict the best time for exploration or settlement. By charting the movement of celestial bodies, they created a celestial navigation system that is still used by modern sailors.

Contributions to Astrophysics

Modern astrophysics owes much to the work of minorities in the field. For instance, Subrahmanyan Chandrasekhar, an Indian astrophysicist, made significant contributions to our understanding of the evolution and structure of stars. He introduced the concept of Chandrasekhar limit, which describes the maximum mass of a stable white dwarf star. This concept is crucial in understanding stellar evolution and the ultimate fate of stars.

Mathematical Innovations

Minority mathematicians have also made significant breakthroughs throughout history. Benjamin Banneker, an African American mathematician, created almanacs with highly accurate astronomical and tidal information. His calculations were used by farmers, sailors, and astronomers for many years. He was also heavily involved in surveying and mapping, using mathematical principles to accurately measure and map areas.

Modern Indigenous Contributions

In modern times, Indigenous cultures continue to contribute to both astronomy and mathematics. For example, the Māori people of New Zealand have incorporated their traditional knowledge of the stars into contemporary astronomical research. They have named a constellation, "Aotearoa," which represents their country and have been actively involved in mapping stars to preserve their cultural heritage.

Unconventional Approach: Native American Sky Stories

One unconventional but valuable approach to teaching astronomy and mathematics is through Native American sky stories. These stories connect celestial phenomena with cultural perspectives and provide a unique way of understanding complex astronomical concepts. By incorporating storytelling into the curriculum, students can develop a deeper appreciation for the contributions of Native American cultures in both astronomy and mathematics.

In conclusion, minority communities have made significant contributions to both astronomy and mathematics throughout history. From ancient knowledge systems to modern innovations, their insights have shaped our understanding of the universe. By recognizing and celebrating these contributions, we can promote a more inclusive and comprehensive narrative of the history of these disciplines.

Section 2: Latin American Influence on American Culture

Subsection 1: Latinx Art and Visual Culture in the United States

Latinx art and visual culture in the United States have a deep and rich history that reflects the diverse experiences and influences of this vibrant community. From traditional art forms rooted in Latin American heritage to contemporary expressions of identity and activism, Latinx artists have made significant contributions to the art world. In this section, we will explore the various forms and themes of Latinx art, the cultural significance behind them, and the artists who have shaped this important facet of American visual culture.

The Evolution of Latinx Art in the United States

Latinx art in the United States has evolved over time, influenced by historical events, social movements, and the intersection of different cultural traditions. It encompasses a wide range of artistic forms, including painting, sculpture, printmaking, photography, performance art, and new media.

One notable period in the history of Latinx art is the Chicano Art Movement of the 1960s and 1970s. Emerging from the civil rights struggles of Mexican Americans, Chicano artists explored themes of identity, cultural heritage, and social justice in their works. Through vibrant murals, graphic prints, and other forms of public art, they sought to reclaim their history and challenge existing power structures.

In more recent years, Latinx artists have expanded upon these foundations and developed their own unique styles and approaches. Many contemporary Latinx artists incorporate elements from both their Latin American roots and their experiences as Latinx individuals living in the United States. This fusion of cultures creates a dynamic and multifaceted body of work that speaks to the complexities of Latinx identity.

Themes in Latinx Art

Latinx art explores a wide range of themes, reflecting the diverse experiences and perspectives within the community. Some common themes include:

- **Identity and Heritage:** Many Latinx artists use their work to explore notions of identity, both personal and collective. They investigate questions of self-identification, cultural heritage, and the intersectionality of their Latinx identity with other aspects of their lives.

- **Social Justice and Activism:** Latinx artists often address social and political issues in their work. They use their art as a form of activism, shedding light on issues such as immigration, racism, and inequality. Through powerful imagery and thought-provoking messages, they seek to provoke dialogue and inspire change.

- **Memory and History:** Latinx art frequently engages with the collective memory and history of Latinx communities. Artists explore the legacies of colonization, cultural assimilation, and the complexities of navigating multiple histories.

- **Borderlands and Transnationalism:** The concept of the border, both physical and metaphorical, is a recurring theme in Latinx art. Artists often explore the experience of living in the borderlands, navigating multiple cultures, languages, and identities. They challenge notions of borders and question the divisions they create.

- **Gender and Sexuality:** Latinx artists often explore themes of gender and sexuality, challenging normative narratives and embracing diverse identities. They examine the intersections of gender, sexuality, race, and culture, highlighting the lived experiences of LGBTQ+ individuals within Latinx communities.

Prominent Latinx Artists

Numerous Latinx artists have made significant contributions to the art world, shaping the discourse and aesthetics of contemporary visual culture. Here are a few examples of prominent Latinx artists and their notable works:

- **Frida Kahlo (1907-1954):** Known for her iconic self-portraits, Frida Kahlo is one of the most celebrated Latinx artists. Through her powerful and introspective paintings, she explored themes of identity, pain, and resilience, becoming an emblematic figure of Mexican and feminist art.
- **Carmen Lomas Garza (b. 1948):** Carmen Lomas Garza is a Mexican American artist known for her vibrant and culturally rich artworks. Her paintings depict the daily life and traditions of Mexican American communities, preserving and celebrating their heritage.
- **Kara Walker (b. 1969):** Kara Walker is an African American artist whose work addresses the intersections of race, gender, and power. Through her large-scale silhouette cutouts, she critically examines the legacy of slavery and its ongoing impact on American society.
- **El Anatsui (b. 1944):** El Anatsui, originally from Ghana, is renowned for his monumental sculptures made from recycled materials such as bottle caps and aluminum cans. His shimmering metallic works explore themes of globalization, consumerism, and African cultural heritage.
- **Ana Mendieta (1948-1985):** Ana Mendieta was a Cuban American artist who used her body as a medium to explore themes of identity, nature, and spirituality. Her groundbreaking performances and earthworks marked a significant contribution to the feminist and land art movements.

Resources and Further Reading

If you are interested in learning more about Latinx art and visual culture, there are numerous resources available to deepen your understanding. Some recommended books and publications include:

- *Del arte chicano al arte chicana* by Carlos Francisco Jackson
- *Homecoming: The Art and Life of William H. Johnson* by Richard J. Powell
- *Latinx Art: Artists, Markets, and Politics* edited by Arlene Dávila
- *Translating Empire: José Martí, Migrant Latino Subjects, and American Modernities* by Laura Lomas
- *Chicana and Chicano Art: Protestarte* edited by Carlos Francisco Jackson

Additionally, visiting museums and galleries that feature Latinx art can provide a firsthand experience of the variety and richness of this artistic expression. Exploring local communities and grasping the cultural context through festivals, exhibitions, and local publications can also deepen your appreciation for Latinx art.

Unconventional Artistic Expressions

Beyond traditional forms of artistic expression, Latinx artists have embraced new media, digital platforms, and unconventional materials to challenge and expand the boundaries of art. For example, some artists use social media platforms as a means of creating and sharing their work, amplifying their voices and reaching broader audiences.

Other artists incorporate found objects, textiles, and multimedia installations into their practice, blurring the lines between art and everyday life. By pushing the boundaries of artistic mediums and exploring new technologies, Latinx artists continue to redefine and reshape the art world.

Conclusion

Latinx art and visual culture in the United States are dynamic and transformative, offering a unique perspective on identity, history, and social justice. From the bold murals of the Chicano Art Movement to the experimental installations of contemporary artists, Latinx art reflects the rich tapestry of experiences within the Latinx community.

By exploring the themes, evolution, and prominent artists in Latinx art, we have just scratched the surface of this vast and diverse field. We encourage you to delve deeper, explore the work of individual artists, and discover the stories and voices embedded in Latinx art. Through engaging with Latinx art, we can cultivate a greater appreciation for the contributions and resilience of this vibrant cultural community in the United States.

Subsection 2: Hispanic Literature and Latin American Magical Realism

Hispanic literature encompasses a rich and diverse body of work that spans centuries and showcases the unique cultural experiences and perspectives of Latin American writers. One distinctive genre within Hispanic literature is known as Magical Realism, which emerged in the mid-20th century and has since become a hallmark of Latin American literary tradition. In this subsection, we will explore the origins, characteristics, and impact of Magical Realism, as well as highlight some notable authors and their works.

Origins of Magical Realism

Magical Realism originated in Latin American literature in the 1940s and 1950s as a response to the prevailing European and North American literary traditions. Writers, such as Gabriel Garcia Marquez from Colombia and Jorge Luis Borges from Argentina, sought to explore the unique cultural and historical experiences of their respective countries through a distinct narrative style. They embraced the blending of the real and the fantastic, the ordinary and the extraordinary, resulting in the emergence of Magical Realism as a prominent literary movement.

Characteristics of Magical Realism

Magical Realism is characterized by its seamless fusion of the ordinary and the magical, blurring the lines between reality and fantasy. It often features elements such as dream-like sequences, supernatural occurrences, and magical beings coexisting with the everyday world. Unlike traditional fantasy or science fiction, Magical Realism does not rely on explicit explanations for these fantastical elements; instead, they are presented as a matter-of-fact part of the narrative. This unique narrative technique allows authors to use magical elements as metaphors for social, political, and cultural issues, providing a deeper understanding of the human experience.

Notable Authors and Works

One of the most celebrated authors in the realm of Magical Realism is Gabriel Garcia Marquez, whose novel "One Hundred Years of Solitude" (1967) is considered a masterpiece of the genre. Set in the fictional town of Macondo, the novel tells the story of the Buendia family across multiple generations, blending myth and reality to depict the tumultuous history of Latin America. Marquez's lyrical prose and imaginative storytelling captivate readers, while his exploration of love, time, and solitude resonates on a universal level.

Another notable figure in Magical Realism is Isabel Allende, whose novel "The House of the Spirits" (1982) embraces elements of magical realism while delving into themes of familial and political turmoil. Allende's work combines elements of fantasy and myth, highlighting the power of storytelling and emphasizing the interconnectedness of past, present, and future.

In addition to Marquez and Allende, other influential authors in the realm of Magical Realism include Julio Cortazar, Laura Esquivel, and Mario Vargas Llosa. Each writer brings their unique perspective and storytelling style to the genre, contributing to the richness and diversity of Hispanic literature.

Impact and Legacy

The impact of Magical Realism extends beyond the realm of literature. It has influenced various art forms, including visual arts, film, and theater. Its blending of reality and fiction, its exploration of cultural identity, and its bold use of symbolism and metaphor have inspired countless artists and creators worldwide.

Furthermore, Magical Realism has played a crucial role in challenging traditional Western literary canons, offering a fresh perspective and highlighting the importance of diverse voices in literature. By incorporating elements of indigenous folklore, mythology, and history, Magical Realism allows Latin American authors to reclaim their cultural heritage and reshape the narrative of their countries.

In conclusion, Magical Realism stands as a testament to the power of storytelling and the rich cultural heritage of Latin America. Through its unique blending of the ordinary and the magical, it has provided a platform for Hispanic writers to express their cultural, historical, and political experiences. It continues to captivate audiences and inspire readers to explore the boundaries of reality, making it an essential genre within Hispanic literature.

Subsection 3: Latinx Contributions to Music and Dance

Latinx culture has had a profound impact on the world of music and dance. From lively rhythms and passionate melodies to energetic movements and intricate choreography, Latinx contributions have enriched and diversified the global music and dance scene. In this section, we will explore the vibrant history and significant contributions of Latinx artists, highlighting their influence and lasting legacy.

Latinx Music Traditions

Latinx music is a tapestry woven from diverse cultural threads, encompassing various genres and styles. One prominent genre is salsa, which originated in the 1960s in New York City and draws influences from Afro-Cuban rhythms, Puerto Rican bomba and plena, and other Latin American musical traditions. Salsa quickly became a worldwide phenomenon, capturing the hearts and igniting the dance floors of people from different backgrounds.

Merengue, another popular Latinx genre, originated in the Dominican Republic. Known for its fast-paced rhythms, accordion melodies, and infectious beats, merengue has become a staple in Latin American and Caribbean music. Artists like Juan Luis Guerra and Johnny Ventura have popularized merengue globally, making it an integral part of Latinx cultural expression.

Cumbia, a rhythmic and melodic genre with roots in Colombia, has also played an essential role in Latinx music. With its origins in African, Indigenous, and European traditions, cumbia combines traditional instruments like the gaita flute, drums, and maracas with modern elements to create a groovy and danceable sound. Artists like Selena Quintanilla and Grupo Niche have propelled cumbia into the mainstream, ensuring its enduring popularity.

Influence on Dance Styles

Latinx music is intricately connected to various dance styles that have captivated audiences worldwide. One prominent dance style is salsa, which emerged as a fusion of Latin American and Afro-Caribbean dances. Characterized by intricate footwork, sensual movements, and partner work, salsa has become an iconic dance form that embodies the spirit and passion of Latinx culture. From social gatherings to international competitions, salsa has gained immense popularity, inspiring dancers and choreographers globally.

Bachata, originating from the Dominican Republic, is another Latinx dance style that has gained international recognition. Known for its heartfelt and romantic nature, bachata features smooth body isolations, sensual hip movements, and intimate partner connections. This dance form has evolved over the years, incorporating modern elements while staying true to its traditional roots. Artists like Romeo Santos and Aventura have ushered bachata into the mainstream, expanding its reach beyond Latinx communities.

In addition to salsa and bachata, Latinx culture has also influenced other popular dance styles such as cha-cha-cha, mambo, and tango. These dances showcase the creativity, elegance, and passionate expressions that are synonymous with Latinx music and dance.

Cross-Cultural Collaborations

Latinx artists have also made significant contributions to cross-cultural collaborations, merging Latinx music with other genres to create exciting fusions. These collaborations have resulted in groundbreaking musical movements and found immense popularity among diverse audiences.

One notable example is reggaeton, a genre that emerged in Puerto Rico in the late 1990s. Combining elements of reggae, hip-hop, and Latin American music, reggaeton has become a global phenomenon, dominated by artists like Daddy Yankee, Bad Bunny, and J Balvin. Through their innovative sounds, they have introduced Latinx music to mainstream platforms, bridging cultural divides and fostering a sense of unity among different communities.

Latinx artists have also infused their cultural heritage into contemporary pop music, creating a fusion of Latin and mainstream sounds. Artists like Shakira, Jennifer Lopez, and Ricky Martin have achieved worldwide success, showcasing the vibrancy and diversity of Latinx music.

Preserving Cultural Identity

While Latinx contributions to music and dance continue to evolve, it is crucial to recognize and preserve cultural identity. Within the Latinx community, efforts are being made to maintain traditional music and dance forms, ensuring that they are passed down to future generations.

Organizations and cultural centers play a vital role in providing platforms for Latinx artists and promoting their contributions. They organize festivals, workshops, and performances that celebrate and educate audiences about the rich heritage of Latinx music and dance.

It is also essential to support and patronize Latinx artists and musicians, not only through listening to their music or attending their concerts but also by advocating for their recognition and fair representation in the music industry. By acknowledging and embracing Latinx contributions to music and dance, we contribute to a more inclusive and culturally diverse society.

Conclusion

Latinx contributions to music and dance have left an indelible mark on cultural expression worldwide. From salsa and merengue to bachata and reggaeton, the infectious rhythms and captivating movements have enchanted audiences around the globe. As we celebrate Latinx music and dance, it is crucial to appreciate the rich heritage, cultural diversity, and significant contributions made by Latinx artists. Through their talents, they have united people across borders, fostering cultural exchange and appreciation. Let us continue to honor and support Latinx artists, ensuring that their contributions continue to flourish and inspire generations to come.

Subsection 4: Immigration and the Latinx Experience in America

The Latinx experience in America is deeply intertwined with the history of immigration. The Latinx community is diverse, comprising individuals from various countries in Latin America, each with their own unique cultures, languages, and traditions. This subsection explores the immigration patterns of Latinx individuals and the challenges they have faced, as well as the contributions they have made to American society.

Latinx Immigration Patterns

Latinx immigration to the United States has a complex history that spans several centuries. While the majority of Latinx individuals in the U.S. today come from Mexico, there are also significant populations from countries such as Puerto Rico, Dominican Republic, Cuba, El Salvador, Guatemala, Colombia, and many others.

Historically, Latinx immigration can be divided into several waves. The first wave occurred in the early 20th century when Mexican workers were recruited to fill labor shortages in industries such as agriculture and railroad construction. This period of mass migration was known as the Mexican Repatriation, during which many Mexican immigrants were subjected to discriminatory policies and forced to return to Mexico.

The second wave of Latinx immigration took place in the mid-20th century, primarily driven by political and economic factors. Many individuals from Cuba and the Dominican Republic sought refuge in the U.S. to escape political instability and oppressive regimes. Additionally, economic hardships in countries like Mexico and Central American nations pushed individuals to seek better opportunities in the U.S.

The most recent wave of Latinx immigration began in the late 20th century and continues to the present day. Factors such as globalization, economic disparities, and violence in their home countries have motivated individuals from various Latin American countries to seek a better life in the U.S. Some Latinx individuals come to the U.S. with legal documentation, while others enter without proper documentation, often referred to as undocumented immigrants.

Challenges Faced by Latinx Immigrants

Latinx immigrants face numerous challenges upon their arrival in the United States. Language barriers can make it difficult for them to access education, healthcare, and employment opportunities. Discrimination and prejudice also pose significant obstacles, with Latinx individuals often facing stereotypes, exclusion, and unfair treatment due to their ethnicity.

Undocumented Latinx immigrants face unique challenges, living in constant fear of deportation and exploitation. They often encounter difficulties in accessing basic services, such as healthcare and education, and are vulnerable to labor exploitation due to their legal status.

Furthermore, the Latinx immigrant community often faces family separation as a result of immigration policies. Many individuals leave their home countries, leaving behind their families and support networks, in pursuit of better opportunities. The challenges of adjusting to a new culture, adapting to a different educational system, and finding stable employment further add to the hardships faced by Latinx immigrants.

Contributions of Latinx Immigrants

Latinx immigrants have made significant contributions in various fields, enriching American society in numerous ways. In the realm of arts and culture, Latinx individuals have brought vibrant forms of expression, including visual arts, literature, music, and dance. Their creativity and unique perspectives have shaped the cultural landscape of the United States, leading to the emergence of influential artists, writers, and performers.

Latinx immigrants have also made substantial contributions in academia, science, and technology. Many Latinx individuals have excelled in higher education, becoming scholars, scientists, engineers, and innovators in various fields. Their achievements have advanced knowledge and propelled scientific and technological advancements.

In the realm of business and entrepreneurship, Latinx immigrants have established successful enterprises, creating job opportunities and contributing to economic growth. Their diverse perspectives, work ethic, and entrepreneurial spirit have played a vital role in shaping the American economy.

Additionally, Latinx immigrants have enriched American cuisine with their traditional dishes and culinary practices. These food traditions have become a significant part of American culture, with Latinx-owned restaurants and food establishments contributing to the culinary landscape of the nation.

The Latinx Experience in America: Challenges and Progress

While Latinx immigrants have made remarkable contributions to American society, they continue to face challenges and barriers. Structural inequalities, discriminatory policies, and xenophobia limit their opportunities for upward social mobility and integration into mainstream society.

However, there have been notable strides towards achieving social justice and inclusivity for Latinx individuals. Advocacy organizations, community initiatives, and social movements have played a crucial role in fighting for immigrant rights and challenging discriminatory practices. The Latinx community, along with allies, has been instrumental in mobilizing for comprehensive immigration reform and advocating for equitable treatment.

In recent years, there has been increased recognition of the contributions and resilience of Latinx immigrants, leading to efforts to promote their inclusion and celebrate their heritage. Educational institutions, non-profit organizations, and governmental bodies have recognized the importance of teaching accurate and inclusive histories that highlight the diverse experiences of Latinx individuals.

Furthermore, Latinx immigrants themselves have played an active role in preserving their cultures, languages, and traditions. Community organizations and grassroots movements contribute to the preservation and promotion of Latinx cultural heritage and identity.

As the Latinx population continues to grow and diversify in the United States, it is vital to address the systemic barriers that hinder their full participation and advancement. By fostering an inclusive and welcoming society, recognizing their contributions, and promoting equitable opportunities, we can create a stronger and more vibrant nation that fully values the Latinx experience.

Conclusion

The immigration and Latinx experience in America are deeply intertwined. Latinx immigrants have faced numerous challenges, including discrimination, language barriers, and family separation. However, they have also made significant contributions to American society in various domains, including arts and culture, academia, science and technology, business, and culinary traditions. Despite the progress made, there is still much work to be done in addressing systemic inequalities and creating an inclusive and equitable society. By recognizing and celebrating the contributions of Latinx immigrants and advocating for their rights, we can foster a more diverse, vibrant, and just America.

Chapter 7: Native American Contributions and Resilience

Section 1: Indigenous Knowledge and Environmental Stewardship

Subsection 1: Indigenous Ecological Wisdom and Conservation

Indigenous cultures around the world have developed profound wisdom and knowledge about their local ecosystems. Their practices and beliefs are deeply rooted in the understanding that humans are an integral part of nature, and that the well-being of the natural world is inextricably linked to the well-being of human communities. In this subsection, we will explore the indigenous ecological wisdom and conservation practices that have sustained habitats and ecosystems for generations.

Indigenous Knowledge Systems

Indigenous knowledge systems are holistic frameworks that integrate social, cultural, and environmental aspects of life. They have evolved over centuries of observation, experimentation, and intergenerational knowledge transfer. Indigenous peoples understand their environment in a way that is both practical and spiritual, recognizing the interconnectedness of all living beings.

These knowledge systems are often based on oral traditions, passed down through storytelling, rituals, and ceremonies. They encompass a deep understanding of ecological processes, plant and animal behaviors, and the intricate balance of ecosystems. Indigenous knowledge systems are also rich in traditional practices, such as sustainable agriculture, land management, and resource conservation.

Traditional Ecological Knowledge

Traditional Ecological Knowledge (TEK) refers to the cumulative body of knowledge, practices, and beliefs held by indigenous communities about their environment. It encompasses a wide range of topics, including weather patterns, animal behavior, medicinal plants, and sustainable resource use.

TEK is rooted in a deep connection to the land and the belief that humans are stewards of nature. Indigenous peoples have developed sophisticated strategies to maintain the health and productivity of ecosystems while meeting their own needs. These strategies often involve the careful observation of natural indicators, such as the behavior of animal species, the flowering of certain plants, or changes in weather patterns.

For example, indigenous communities in North America have long practiced controlled burning to manage forested landscapes. They understand that fire can be a vital ecological process, promoting healthy growth and reducing the risk of catastrophic wildfires. By intentionally setting fires at specific times and in certain areas, they maintain the diversity of plant and animal species, regenerate nutrients in the soil, and clear away underbrush that could fuel larger fires.

Conservation Practices

Indigenous peoples have developed a range of conservation practices that allow them to sustainably manage their natural resources. These practices are often deeply ingrained in their cultural and spiritual traditions, reinforcing a sense of responsibility and respect for the environment.

One example of indigenous conservation practice is the concept of "resource guardianship." Indigenous communities act as custodians of their local ecosystems, ensuring the sustainable use of natural resources for future generations. This includes enforcing fishing and hunting restrictions, protecting sacred sites, and participating in ecological restoration efforts.

Additionally, indigenous communities have long practiced rotational farming or shifting cultivation. This sustainable agricultural method involves periodically moving agricultural activities to new areas, allowing previously used land to regenerate and maintaining soil fertility. By adopting this practice, indigenous peoples promote biodiversity, prevent soil erosion, and preserve the long-term productivity of their lands.

Challenges and Future Outlook

Despite their valuable contributions to ecological wisdom and conservation, indigenous communities face numerous challenges in maintaining their traditional practices. Encroachment on their lands, forced relocation, and loss of cultural autonomy disrupt the delicate balance between human societies and their environment.

However, there is growing recognition of the importance of indigenous ecological wisdom and the need to protect indigenous rights and territories. Collaborative efforts between indigenous communities, researchers, and policymakers are vital in order to support and promote the sustainable practices and knowledge systems of indigenous peoples.

By integrating indigenous ecological wisdom and conservation practices into mainstream environmental management, we can learn valuable lessons about sustainable resource use, ecosystem restoration, and our interconnectedness with the natural world. It is crucial that we recognize and respect the immense contributions of indigenous communities, not only for the preservation of biodiversity but also for the well-being of our planet and future generations.

Case Study: The Haida People and the Haida Gwaii Watchmen

The Haida people of Haida Gwaii, an archipelago off the coast of British Columbia, Canada, have a deep spiritual and ecological connection to their ancestral lands. With their profound knowledge of the local ecosystems, the Haida have played a crucial role in protecting their environment and preserving their cultural heritage.

The Haida Gwaii Watchmen program is a shining example of indigenous ecological wisdom and conservation in action. This program, initiated by the Haida Nation, involves the employment of local Haida as cultural guardians who monitor and protect ancient village sites and fragile ecosystems on Haida Gwaii.

The Haida Gwaii Watchmen work to maintain the delicate balance between tourism and environmental preservation. They educate visitors about the cultural significance of the sites and the importance of sustainable practices. By doing so, they not only promote the preservation of their cultural heritage but also serve as ambassadors for the protection of their lands and waters.

The success of the Haida Gwaii Watchmen program not only showcases the effectiveness of indigenous ecological wisdom and conservation practices but also highlights the importance of empowering indigenous communities in the management of their ancestral lands. This case study serves as an inspiration and a model for how we can collaborate with indigenous peoples to protect our planet's rich biodiversity and cultural heritage.

Additional Resources

- Smith, L. T. (2005). Decolonizing methodologies: Research and indigenous peoples. Zed Books. - Berkes, F. (2012). Sacred ecology. Routledge. - Turner, N. J., & Berkes, F. (Eds.). (2006). Coming to grips with nature: Pathways to a sustainable future. University of Manitoba Press. - Battiste, M., & Henderson, J. Y. (2000). Protecting Indigenous knowledges and heritage: A global challenge. UBC press. - Toledo, V. M., & Barrera-Bassols, N. (2017). Ancestral wisdom and ecosystem science for the future of humanity. Ecology and Society, 22(1).

Exercises

1. Research and share an example of an indigenous ecological practice from a culture in your region. Discuss its significance and the benefits it provides for both the environment and the community.

2. Discuss the challenges faced by indigenous communities in maintaining their traditional ecological knowledge and conservation practices. What can be done to support and protect these practices?

3. Explore the concept of rotational farming or shifting cultivation. How does this practice contribute to sustainable agriculture and the preservation of biodiversity? Provide examples from different regions of the world.

4. Reflect on your own relationship with the natural world. How can you incorporate indigenous ecological wisdom and conservation practices into your daily life? Discuss specific actions you can take to promote sustainability and respect for the environment.

Subsection 2: Native American Agricultural Practices

Agriculture played a crucial role in the development and sustenance of Native American communities for thousands of years. Native American agricultural practices were not only innovative but also deeply connected to their cultural and spiritual beliefs. In this section, we will explore the fascinating methods and principles behind Native American agricultural practices.

Traditional Farming Techniques

Native American farmers practiced a variety of techniques to cultivate their crops. One such technique was known as companion planting, where different crops were planted together to enhance growth and deter pests. For example, the "Three Sisters" method, used by several Native American tribes, involved planting corn, beans, and squash together. Corn provided support for the beans to climb, beans added nitrogen to the soil, and squash acted as ground cover, preventing weed growth and moisture loss.

Another technique used by Native American farmers was terracing, the construction of small, levelled platforms on hillsides. These terraces helped retain water, prevent soil erosion, and create microclimates suitable for different crops. The ability to grow crops on steep slopes was essential in regions with limited arable land.

Crop Diversity and Sustainability

Native American agriculture was characterized by its remarkable crop diversity. Native farmers cultivated numerous varieties of corn, beans, squash, sunflower, amaranth, and many other crops. This diversity not only provided nutritional security but also minimized the risk of crop failure due to pests, diseases, or environmental factors.

Furthermore, Native American agricultural practices prioritized sustainability. They implemented systems such as crop rotation, allowing the soil to replenish its nutrients naturally. Some tribes also practiced fallowing, in which farmland was left uncultivated for certain periods to restore its fertility.

Water Management

Water management was crucial for Native American agricultural success, especially in arid regions. Tribes implemented various irrigation techniques to efficiently distribute water to their fields. One such technique was the construction of canals or ditches to divert water from rivers or other water sources to agricultural lands. These canals often incorporated sophisticated engineering principles to control the flow of water.

In addition to irrigation, Native American farmers were skilled in capturing and storing rainwater. They built stone-lined or earthen reservoirs known as "waffle gardens" to collect and retain water during the rainy season. This technique allowed them to grow crops sustainably even in areas with limited rainfall.

Cultural and Spiritual Significance

Native American agricultural practices had profound cultural and spiritual significance. Farming was viewed as a sacred act, deeply interconnected with the earth and the well-being of the community. Rituals and ceremonies were performed to honor the spirits of the land, seek blessings for bountiful harvests, and express gratitude for the abundance provided by Mother Earth.

For example, the Pueblo tribes of the Southwest had elaborate ceremonies to invoke rain and ensure successful crop growth. These rituals involved dances, music, prayers, and the offering of cornmeal to deities associated with agriculture.

Challenges and Contemporary Significance

Despite the immense contributions of Native American agricultural practices, these traditional methods have faced challenges over time. Historical events, such as forced relocation and colonization, disrupted traditional farming practices and eroded knowledge systems. The introduction of European farming techniques also led to the loss of indigenous knowledge and sustainability practices.

However, in recent years, there has been a resurgence of interest in Native American agricultural practices. Recognizing their resilience, environmental sustainability, and nutritional benefits, many indigenous communities are reviving traditional farming methods. These practices not only promote food sovereignty but also preserve cultural heritage and foster community cohesion.

Example: The Oneida Nation and Sustainable Agriculture

The Oneida Nation, located in Wisconsin, United States, is a prime example of a Native American community embracing sustainable agriculture. They have implemented a range of innovative techniques to foster ecological balance and promote community well-being.

One initiative is the Turtle Gardens project, where community members grow traditional crops, such as corn, beans, and squash, using organic and sustainable practices. The project emphasizes intergenerational knowledge transfer, with elders passing down traditional agricultural wisdom to younger generations.

Additionally, the Oneida Nation has established a bison herd as part of their regenerative agriculture efforts. The bison provide ecological benefits, such as restoring prairie ecosystems and promoting biodiversity, while also contributing to the community's food security and cultural revitalization.

By combining traditional knowledge with contemporary sustainable farming practices, the Oneida Nation showcases the power of Native American agricultural practices in addressing social, cultural, and environmental challenges.

Further Resources

To delve deeper into Native American agricultural practices, the following resources are highly recommended:

- Book: "Braiding Sweetgrass: Indigenous Wisdom, Scientific Knowledge, and the Teachings of Plants" by Robin Wall Kimmerer. This book beautifully explores the connections between indigenous wisdom and ecology.
- Documentary: "Seeds of Time." This thought-provoking documentary explores the importance of preserving crop diversity and the role of indigenous communities in maintaining food security.
- Website: Traditional Native American Farmers Association (TNAFA). TNAFA is a non-profit organization that supports indigenous farmers and promotes sustainable agriculture through education and advocacy. Their website provides valuable information and resources on Native American agricultural practices.

By studying and appreciating Native American agricultural practices, we gain not only a deeper understanding of their contributions to history but also valuable insights into sustainable farming techniques that can inspire and guide us towards a more resilient and harmonious future.

Subsection 3: Medicinal Plants and Healing Traditions

Throughout history, indigenous cultures and Native American communities have relied on the abundant resources provided by nature to maintain their health and well-being. Medicinal plants and healing traditions have played a crucial role in their healthcare practices, addressing various ailments and promoting overall wellness. In this subsection, we will explore the rich diversity of medicinal plants used by Native Americans and delve into their healing traditions.

Traditional Knowledge of Medicinal Plants

Native American cultures have an extensive understanding of the local flora and its medicinal properties. Passed down through generations, this traditional knowledge encompasses the identification, preparation, and application of medicinal plants for different health conditions.

For example, the Cherokee tribe of the southeastern United States has a long-standing tradition of using plants like Echinacea and blackberry to treat infections and promote healing. They also utilize plants such as prickly pear cactus and sagebrush for their anti-inflammatory properties.

Herbal Remedies

Herbal remedies derived from medicinal plants are a fundamental part of Native American healing traditions. These remedies often involve the preparation of infusions, tinctures, poultices, or salves.

One such example is the use of yarrow by the Navajo tribe. Yarrow leaves are used to create poultices, applied topically to stop bleeding and promote wound healing. Additionally, the leaves can be brewed into a tea to alleviate symptoms of digestive issues and fever.

Sweat Lodge Ceremonies

Sweat lodge ceremonies are a significant aspect of Native American healing traditions. These ceremonies involve the use of medicinal plants, such as sage, cedar, and sweetgrass, to create a sacred and healing environment.

During these ceremonies, participants gather in a small enclosed space and are exposed to intense heat generated by heated rocks. Water infused with medicinal plants is poured over the rocks, releasing steam that promotes intense sweating and detoxification. This practice is believed to cleanse the body and facilitate physical, emotional, and spiritual healing.

Collaboration with Western Medicine

In recent years, there has been a growing recognition of the value of traditional healing practices, including the use of medicinal plants, by contemporary healthcare systems. Collaborative efforts between Native American healers and Western medicine practitioners have led to an integrated approach to healthcare.

For instance, in some Native American communities, healers work alongside medical professionals to incorporate traditional healing practices into standard medical treatments. This collaboration acknowledges the strengths of both systems and offers patients a holistic and culturally sensitive approach to healthcare.

Challenges and Conservation

Despite the significant contributions of medicinal plants and healing traditions to healthcare, there are challenges that need to be addressed. One such challenge is the loss of traditional knowledge due to urbanization, assimilation, and the impact of colonization.

Efforts are being made to preserve and protect traditional knowledge and the medicinal plants themselves. Initiatives that promote sustainable harvesting practices, cultivation of medicinal plants, and the documentation of traditional healing practices are essential for the preservation of these invaluable resources.

Case Study: Traditional Healing Practices in the Southwest

To illustrate the practical application of medicinal plants and healing traditions, let's examine a specific case study: traditional healing practices in the Southwest region of the United States.

Among the Navajo and Apache tribes, the concept of hózh⊠,⊠which means "harmony" or "beauty," forms the foundation of their healing practices. Medicinal plants such as yucca, juniper, and greenthread are used to restore balance in the body and promote overall well-being.

In the Southwest, ceremonies, such as the Blessingway, and the use of sacred plants like white sage, play a crucial role in healing rituals. These practices embody the interconnectedness between physical health, spiritual well-being, and the natural world.

Conclusion

Medicinal plants and healing traditions are a testament to the wisdom and resilience of Native American communities. Their knowledge of the natural world and effective use of medicinal plants offer valuable insights and potential solutions to contemporary healthcare challenges.

By acknowledging and respecting the contributions of indigenous cultures, we can foster a more inclusive and comprehensive approach to healthcare that embraces the healing wisdom embedded in medicinal plants and traditional healing practices. Let us strive to integrate and learn from these diverse practices, ensuring their preservation for future generations.

Subsection 4: Indigenous Views on Land and Resource Management

Land and resource management is a complex and essential part of sustaining our environment. Indigenous communities have long recognized the importance of preserving and responsibly using natural resources. Their views on land and resource management are deeply rooted in a holistic understanding of the environment and the interconnectedness of all living beings. In this subsection, we will explore some of the key principles and practices followed by indigenous communities in managing land and resources.

Principles of Indigenous Land Stewardship

Central to indigenous views on land and resource management is the belief that humans are an integral part of nature and must live in harmony with it. This worldview emphasizes the importance of maintaining a balanced relationship with the natural world, rather than exploiting it for short-term gain. Indigenous communities view land as a sacred entity with inherent rights, rather than a commodity to be bought and sold. This perspective recognizes the value of traditional ecological knowledge and respects the role of indigenous peoples as custodians of the land.

Indigenous land stewardship is guided by several principles, including:

- **Sustainability**: Indigenous communities prioritize sustainable practices that ensure the long-term availability of resources. They understand the interconnectedness of ecosystems and the need to maintain ecological balance.

- **Inter-generational Responsibility**: Indigenous communities recognize that they are caretakers of the land for future generations. They believe in passing down traditional knowledge and teaching younger generations about their responsibilities as stewards of the environment.

- **Community Engagement**: Indigenous land management is often a collective effort that involves the entire community. Decision-making processes are inclusive and consider the needs and perspectives of all community members.

- **Conservation**: Conservation is a central principle in indigenous land management. Indigenous communities have developed strategies to protect biodiversity, preserve natural habitats, and prevent overexploitation of resources.

- **Respect for Indigenous Rights:** Indigenous land management practices respect the inherent rights of indigenous peoples. This includes recognizing and upholding indigenous land tenure systems, ensuring the free, prior, and informed consent of indigenous communities in resource development projects, and respecting indigenous cultural practices and traditions.

Practices of Indigenous Land and Resource Management

Indigenous communities employ a variety of practices to manage land and resources sustainably. These practices have been developed over generations and are deeply rooted in traditional knowledge and cultural values. Here are some examples:

- **Traditional Ecological Knowledge** (TEK): TEK is a body of knowledge developed by indigenous communities through direct observation and experience of the natural environment. It includes an understanding of ecological processes, plant and animal behavior, and the interrelationships between different species. Indigenous communities use TEK to inform land management decisions, such as determining the best time to harvest resources or implementing controlled burning to maintain healthy ecosystems.

- **Fire Management:** Many indigenous communities have practiced controlled burning for centuries as a way to manage ecosystems. Controlled burns help reduce the risk of wildfires, promote the growth of certain plant species, and create a more diverse habitat for wildlife. Indigenous communities have intimate knowledge of the conditions under which controlled burns can be safely conducted and which areas should be prioritized for burning.

- **Resource Rotation:** Indigenous communities often practice resource rotation, where they selectively harvest resources from different areas or at different times to allow for natural replenishment. For example, certain fishing grounds may be closed during specific times of the year to allow fish populations to breed and grow. This practice ensures the sustainability of resources and prevents overexploitation.

- **Regenerative Agriculture:** Indigenous agricultural practices focus on regenerating the soil and maintaining its fertility. These practices include crop rotation, intercropping, and organic farming techniques. Indigenous communities have cultivated a variety of traditional crops that are adapted to local environments, conserving biodiversity and enhancing resilience to climate change.

- **Territorial Management:** Indigenous communities have developed systems for managing their territories effectively. This includes mapping and demarcating boundaries, monitoring resource use, and resolving conflicts over land and resources. These territorial management practices help ensure the sustainability of resources and the preservation of indigenous cultural heritage.

Challenges and the Need for Recognition

Despite the value and effectiveness of indigenous land and resource management practices, many challenges persist. Indigenous communities often face marginalization, discrimination, and land dispossession, which undermine their ability to practice their traditional land stewardship. These challenges threaten not only the rights and well-being of indigenous peoples but also the sustainability of our planet.

Recognition of indigenous knowledge and practices is crucial for addressing these challenges. Governments, policymakers, and non-indigenous communities need to actively engage with and learn from indigenous peoples to develop inclusive and sustainable land management policies. Such recognition can help create a more equitable and environmentally resilient society.

Conclusion

Indigenous views on land and resource management offer valuable insights into how we can build a more sustainable and inclusive future. Their principles of sustainability, inter-generational responsibility, community engagement, conservation, and respect for indigenous rights provide a framework for managing land and resources in a way that respects our planet and its diverse cultures. By recognizing and supporting indigenous land stewardship practices, we can learn from their wisdom and contribute to the well-being of current and future generations.

Section 2: Native American Art, Language, and Cultural Preservation

Subsection 1: Native American Visual Arts and Crafts

Native American visual arts and crafts encompass a rich and diverse range of artistic expressions that reflect the cultural heritage and artistic traditions of Indigenous peoples. These art forms include pottery, basketry, beadwork, weaving, and painting, among others. Through their artwork, Native American artists convey their unique perspectives, stories, and values, while also preserving and celebrating their cultural identities.

Cultural Significance and Symbolism

Native American visual arts and crafts hold deep cultural significance and are often infused with symbolic meaning. They serve as a powerful means of communication and storytelling, connecting the present generation with their ancestors and the natural world. Each artistic element embraces symbolic motifs, colors, and patterns that convey spiritual, historical, and cultural messages.

For instance, pottery is a central art form in many Native American tribes. The designs and motifs on pottery reflect elements of nature, such as animals, plants, and natural landscapes. These motifs often symbolize important cultural concepts, such as fertility, protection, and spiritual beliefs. The choice of colors and patterns on the pottery may also represent different tribes, clans, or personal narratives, creating a visual language that speaks to the uniqueness of each Indigenous community.

Traditional Techniques and Materials

Native American visual arts and crafts are characterized by the meticulous craftsmanship and the use of traditional techniques and materials. The artists employ age-old methods that have been handed down through generations, preserving the authenticity of their cultural heritage.

In pottery-making, for example, artists typically hand-coil the vessels using locally sourced clay. They shape the vessels by coil-building and then smooth the surface using specialized tools. After the shaping process, the artisans apply natural pigments and use various firing techniques to create the desired finish. The use of traditional materials and methods not only ensures the cultural integrity of the artwork but also contributes to the overall aesthetic appeal.

Contemporary Adaptations and Innovations

While Native American visual arts and crafts have deep roots in traditional practices, many contemporary Native American artists are also incorporating modern techniques and materials into their creations. This allows for innovative expressions while still honoring their ancestral traditions.

For instance, some artists have explored new forms of pottery-making by incorporating new designs, colors, and shapes that reflect their evolving cultural identities. Others have incorporated contemporary materials, such as glass beads and metal elements, into traditional beadwork, creating unique and intricate pieces that blend old and new aesthetics.

Preservation and Revitalization Efforts

Preservation and revitalization of Native American visual arts and crafts are crucial to ensure the continuity of these cultural traditions. Many Indigenous communities, educational institutions, museums, and art organizations have been actively involved in preserving and promoting Native American art forms.

Efforts range from providing resources and training to aspiring Native American artists to establishing cultural centers and museums dedicated to showcasing and preserving Indigenous artwork. These initiatives not only contribute to the preservation of traditional art forms but also create opportunities for Native American artists to showcase their work and generate income.

Appreciating and Supporting Native American Art

Appreciating and supporting Native American visual arts and crafts is essential in recognizing the contributions of Indigenous artists and sustaining their cultural practices. Here are some ways individuals can engage with and support Native American art forms:

- Visit Native American art exhibitions, galleries, and cultural centers to learn about and appreciate the diverse range of artwork.

- Purchase authentic Native American art directly from Indigenous artists or reputable sources to ensure fair compensation for their work.

- Educate oneself about the cultural significance and symbolism behind Native American visual arts and crafts to promote respectful engagement.

- Support Native American art organizations and initiatives that work towards preserving and promoting Indigenous art forms.
- Share knowledge and raise awareness about the contributions and artistic achievements of Native American artists within personal and professional networks.

By actively engaging with and supporting Native American visual arts and crafts, individuals can play a vital role in preserving cultural diversity and fostering the continued success and appreciation of Indigenous artistic practices.

Conclusion

Native American visual arts and crafts are a testament to the rich cultural heritage and artistic traditions of Indigenous peoples. Through pottery, basketry, beadwork, weaving, and painting, Native American artists convey their stories, values, and identities while preserving their cultural heritage. These art forms hold deep cultural significance and are infused with symbolic motifs, colors, and patterns that connect the present generation with their ancestors and the natural world. While rooted in traditional techniques and materials, Native American artists also embrace contemporary adaptations and innovations, reflecting their evolving cultural identities. The preservation and revitalization of these art forms depend on the efforts of Indigenous communities, educational institutions, museums, and art organizations. By appreciating and supporting Native American visual arts and crafts, individuals can contribute to the preservation of cultural diversity and the recognition of Indigenous contributions to the broader artistic landscape.

Subsection 2: Native American Languages and Language Revitalization

Native American languages have a rich and diverse history, reflecting the unique cultures and traditions of Indigenous communities across North America. However, these languages are now facing the threat of extinction. The loss of Native American languages has profound implications for the cultural identity, knowledge systems, and spiritual practices of these communities. Language revitalization efforts are essential to preserve and promote the rich linguistic heritage of Native American cultures.

Preserving and Documenting Native American Languages

Preserving and documenting Native American languages is the first step in language revitalization. Linguists work closely with Native communities to record and analyze languages on the brink of extinction. Detailed phonetic transcriptions, grammatical analyses, and dictionaries are created to capture the intricacies of these languages. This documentation not only serves as a valuable resource for language learners but also helps in understanding the unique linguistic features and historical connections of Native American languages.

Challenges in Language Revitalization

Revitalizing endangered Native American languages is a complex task that involves numerous challenges. One significant challenge is the lack of fluent speakers. Many Native American languages suffered a decline due to historical assimilation policies, residential schools, and forced cultural assimilation. The loss of fluent speakers has posed a significant obstacle to language revitalization efforts. However, through the efforts of dedicated community members, educators, and linguists, there has been a renewed interest in language revitalization, with more Native individuals taking active roles in learning, teaching, and promoting their ancestral languages.

Language Immersion Programs

Language immersion programs play a crucial role in Native American language revitalization. These programs provide a supportive and immersive environment for language learners, where they can acquire fluency in the language through everyday conversation, cultural activities, and exposure to Native American traditions. Native communities have established language preservation schools and immersion camps to create spaces where children and adults can learn the language in a comprehensive and culturally relevant manner.

Technology and Language Revitalization

Advancements in technology have played a pivotal role in language revitalization efforts. Mobile applications, online learning platforms, and virtual classrooms have made language learning more accessible to a broader audience. These technological tools allow for interactive language lessons, vocabulary drills, and cultural resources to be easily accessible to language learners. Additionally, social media platforms and online forums provide spaces for language learners to practice and engage with other Native speakers, fostering a sense of community and support in their language journey.

Positive Impacts of Language Revitalization

Language revitalization has numerous positive impacts on Native American communities. First and foremost, it helps to restore and strengthen cultural identity, as language is deeply intertwined with cultural practices, ceremonies, and spiritual beliefs. Revitalizing Native American languages also promotes intergenerational connections, as the transfer of language knowledge between elders and younger generations fosters a sense of belonging and cultural continuity. Furthermore, language revitalization enhances educational opportunities, empowers Native communities to reclaim their heritage, and contributes to the preservation of traditional ecological knowledge.

Resources and Support for Language Revitalization

Various organizations and initiatives provide resources and support for Native American language revitalization efforts. The Endangered Language Fund, the National Indian Education Association, and the Native American Language Institute are among the organizations actively involved in providing funding, training, and technical assistance. Additionally, collaborations between linguists, educators, tribal communities, and governmental agencies have led to the development of comprehensive language revitalization plans and programs.

Exercises

1. Research a Native American language that is currently being revitalized. Identify the linguistic features unique to that language and find resources that support language learning.
2. Create a poster or infographic that highlights the importance of preserving Native American languages and the positive impacts of language revitalization.
3. Interview a fluent speaker of a Native American language to learn about their experiences in language revitalization efforts. Document their insights and share them with your class or community.

Conclusion

The revitalization of Native American languages is a critical endeavor that contributes to the preservation of cultural heritage, community resilience, and knowledge systems. By preserving, documenting, and promoting these languages, we honor the contributions of Indigenous communities and recognize their inherent right to cultural self-determination. Through ongoing language revitalization efforts, we can ensure that Native American languages thrive and continue to enrich our understanding of human history, diversity, and interconnectedness.

Subsection 4: Native American Contributions to Literature and Oral Tradition

Native American literature and oral tradition play a significant role in preserving and transmitting the rich cultural heritage of Indigenous communities. Through storytelling, poetry, and song, Native Americans have conveyed their history, beliefs, and worldview for centuries. This subsection explores the contributions of Native American authors and storytellers, the significance of oral tradition, and the impact of Indigenous literature on contemporary society.

The Power of Oral Tradition

Oral tradition has always been central to Native American culture as a means of passing down knowledge from one generation to another. Native American tribes have used storytelling and oratory skills to share myths, legends, histories, and moral teachings. These oral traditions are not just about the stories themselves, but also about the values, customs, and identity of the tribes.

Oral storytelling allows for flexibility and adaptation, reflecting the dynamic nature of Native American societies. The narratives are often performed in communal settings, fostering community bonds and emphasizing the importance of collective memory. By listening to these stories, individuals learn about their roots, cultural practices, and the experiences of their ancestors.

Native American Literature

In recent decades, Native American literature written in English has gained recognition and acclaim on a global scale. Native American authors have skillfully blended traditional storytelling techniques with Western literary forms to create unique and influential works. These literary contributions have challenged and expanded the canon of American literature, adding diverse voices and perspectives to the literary landscape.

Prominent Native American authors such as Leslie Marmon Silko, Louise Erdrich, Sherman Alexie, and N. Scott Momaday have achieved widespread recognition for their works. Their writing addresses themes of identity, colonialism, spirituality, and the complex relationship between Native Americans and the dominant society. Through their storytelling, these authors shed light on the historical and contemporary struggles faced by Indigenous communities.

Native American literature is characterized by its vivid imagery, lyrical prose, and powerful storytelling. It often incorporates traditional storytelling techniques such as repetition, symbolism, and cyclical narratives. These elements not only make the literature aesthetically engaging but also evoke a sense of cultural continuity and resilience.

Preserving Cultural Heritage

Native American literature serves as a vehicle for preserving and revitalizing Indigenous languages and cultural traditions. Many Native American authors write in both English and their ancestral languages, bridging the gap between generations and preserving endangered languages. Through their literary works, they raise awareness about the importance of language preservation and the cultural richness embedded within these languages.

Additionally, Native American authors provide insights into the social, political, and environmental issues faced by their communities. Their works often challenge stereotypes and misconceptions about Native Americans, promoting a more accurate understanding of Indigenous experience. This counter-narrative exposes readers to different perspectives and fosters empathy and cultural appreciation.

The Influence of Native American Literature

Native American literature has had a profound impact on contemporary society. By amplifying Indigenous voices and experiences, it has contributed to the broader movement for cultural recognition and social justice. Indigenous authors have brought attention to issues such as land rights, environmental degradation, and the legacy of colonization.

Furthermore, Native American literature offers valuable perspectives for readers from all backgrounds. It provides an opportunity to engage with diverse cultures, challenge preconceptions, and foster cross-cultural dialogue. Through exposure to Native American literature, readers can gain a deeper understanding of Indigenous histories, traditions, and contemporary realities.

In classrooms, Native American literature is increasingly being incorporated into curricula to promote cultural diversity and critical thinking. Through the study of these works, students can develop a more nuanced understanding of Indigenous cultures and the power of storytelling as a means of cultural preservation.

Conclusion

Native American literature and oral tradition are essential components of Indigenous identity and cultural resilience. Through storytelling and the written word, Native American authors have preserved their history, challenged stereotypes, and advocated for social justice. By engaging with Native American literature, readers have the opportunity to broaden their horizons, deepen their cultural understanding, and contribute to a more inclusive and diverse society.

Subsection 5: Influence of Native American Music and Dance

Native American music and dance have a rich cultural history that dates back thousands of years. These art forms hold great significance within Native American communities, serving as a means of storytelling, spiritual expression, and cultural preservation. In this section, we will explore the influence of Native American music and dance, highlighting their unique characteristics, cultural importance, and impact on contemporary society.

Traditional Native American Musical Instruments

Native American music is intimately connected with the use of traditional musical instruments that have been passed down through generations. These instruments vary across tribes and regions, but some commonly used ones include:

- **Drums:** The drum is one of the most important instruments in Native American music. It is often made from animal hides stretched over a wooden frame and played with either a beater or hands.

- **Flutes:** Native American flutes are known for their haunting and melodic tones. They are typically made from wood and have a distinctive sound that is often associated with Native American music.

- **Rattles:** Rattles are percussion instruments that are often made from materials such as gourds, shells, or animal bones. They produce a rhythmic and shaking sound, adding texture to Native American music.

These instruments play a significant role in Native American music, providing a rhythmic foundation and enhancing the overall emotional and spiritual impact of the music and dance.

Characteristics of Native American Music

Native American music is deeply rooted in cultural traditions and exhibits several distinctive characteristics:

1. **Vocal Styles:** Native American music often features vocal styles characterized by melodic lines, rhythmic patterns, and intricate ornamentation. Vocals can range from solo performances to layered harmonies, creating a unique and captivating sound.

2. **Rhythmic Complexity:** Rhythm is a fundamental element of Native American music. Complex rhythmic patterns are created using drums, rattles, and other percussive instruments. These rhythms are often syncopated, creating a dynamic and energetic atmosphere.

3. **Nature-Inspired Melodies:** Native American music draws inspiration from the natural world, with melodies reflecting the sounds of nature, such as bird songs and wind patterns. These melodies often carry deep spiritual and cultural meanings.

4. **Call-and-Response Structures:** Many Native American songs are structured as call-and-response, where one singer or group initiates a musical phrase, and others respond with a different but complementary phrase. This creates a sense of community and interaction within the music.

5. **Improvisation and Variation:** Native American music embraces improvisation and variation, allowing musicians and dancers to express their individuality while adhering to the core traditions. This flexibility ensures that the music remains alive and adaptable to contemporary contexts.

Cultural Significance and Contemporary Impact

Native American music and dance hold immense cultural significance and serve multiple purposes within indigenous communities:

- **Preserving Cultural Heritage:** Native American music and dance play a crucial role in preserving and transmitting cultural traditions. They serve as a medium for passing down stories, customs, and spiritual beliefs from one generation to another.

- **Spiritual and Ceremonial Practices:** Music and dance are integral to Native American spiritual and ceremonial practices. They invoke a connection to ancestral spirits, express gratitude to the natural world, and mark important life events, such as coming-of-age ceremonies and harvest celebrations.
- **Community Cohesion:** Music and dance foster a sense of community and belonging within Native American societies. They bring people together, allowing for collective participation and shared experiences, strengthening social bonds and cultural identity.
- **Education and Awareness:** Native American music and dance have become powerful tools for educating the general public about indigenous cultures. Through public performances, recordings, and cultural events, Native American artists and performers promote understanding, respect, and appreciation for their heritage.

The influence of Native American music and dance extends beyond indigenous communities and continues to resonate in contemporary society. Native American artists have made significant contributions to various music genres, including folk, rock, jazz, and hip-hop, incorporating traditional elements into their compositions. Furthermore, Native American dance forms have influenced modern choreography, adding diversity and cultural richness to the world of dance.

Contemporary Challenges and Revitalization Efforts

Despite its enduring cultural significance, Native American music and dance face several challenges:

- **Cultural Appropriation:** Native American music and dance have often been appropriated and misused by non-indigenous individuals and groups, leading to the misrepresentation and commodification of indigenous cultures. This raises concerns about cultural exploitation and the need for respectful engagement.
- **Loss of Traditional Knowledge:** The transmission of traditional musical practices has been hindered by historical factors such as forced assimilation, boarding schools, and cultural suppression. As a result, some traditional knowledge has been lost or is at risk of disappearing.

- **Revitalization Efforts:** Native American communities and organizations are actively engaged in revitalizing their musical traditions. Efforts include cultural education programs, intergenerational knowledge exchange, and collaborations between traditional and contemporary artists.

To address these challenges, it is essential to support and amplify the voices of Native American musicians, dancers, and cultural advocates. By fostering understanding, recognizing cultural rights, and promoting ethical engagement, we can contribute to the preservation and revitalization of Native American music and dance for future generations.

In conclusion, Native American music and dance have a profound influence on cultural heritage, spiritual practices, and community cohesion within indigenous communities. Their unique characteristics and cultural significance continue to shape contemporary music and dance forms. By recognizing and appreciating the contributions of Native American artists, we can celebrate the diversity of human expression and foster greater cultural understanding.

Chapter 8: Contributions and Struggles of Religious Minorities

Section 1: Jewish Contributions to Science, Arts, and Philosophy

Subsection 1: Jewish Nobel Prize Laureates and Scientific Advancements

The Jewish community has made significant contributions to science, leading to numerous Nobel Prize laureates and groundbreaking scientific advancements. Throughout history, Jewish scientists have played a pivotal role in various fields, including physics, chemistry, medicine, and economics. This section highlights some of the notable Jewish Nobel Prize laureates and their scientific achievements.

Physics

One of the most famous Jewish physicists is Albert Einstein. Although he did not receive the Nobel Prize specifically for his Theory of Relativity, his work on the photoelectric effect earned him the Nobel Prize in Physics in 1921. His theory revolutionized the understanding of light and laid the foundation for the development of quantum mechanics.

Another prominent Jewish physicist is Isidor Isaac Rabi, who was awarded the Nobel Prize in Physics in 1944 for his resonance method. Rabi's scientific contributions allowed the precise measurement of magnetic properties of atomic nuclei, leading to the development of nuclear magnetic resonance (NMR) spectroscopy. This technique has become an essential tool in chemistry, physics, and medicine.

Chemistry

Jewish scientists have also made significant advancements in the field of chemistry. One notable example is Fritz Haber, who was awarded the Nobel Prize in Chemistry in 1918 for his development of the Haber-Bosch process. This process revolutionized the production of ammonia, making it possible to produce synthetic fertilizers on a large scale and greatly contributing to global food production.

Another remarkable Jewish chemist is Herbert A. Hauptman, who won the Nobel Prize in Chemistry in 1985. Hauptman developed mathematical methods for determining crystal structures using X-ray diffraction analysis. His pioneering work in crystallography significantly advanced the understanding of molecular structures and played a crucial role in various fields, including drug design and materials science.

Medicine

In the field of medicine, Jewish scientists have made groundbreaking discoveries and advancements. For instance, Paul Ehrlich, known as the "Father of Chemotherapy," received the Nobel Prize in Physiology or Medicine in 1908 for his work on immunology and the development of the first effective treatment for syphilis. Ehrlich's contributions laid the foundation for modern chemotherapy and the use of drugs to target specific pathogens.

Another influential Jewish scientist is Albert Calmette, who, along with his colleague Camille Guérin, developed the Bacillus Calmette-Guérin (BCG) vaccine for tuberculosis. The BCG vaccine, still in use today, has saved countless lives and remains a critical tool in the fight against tuberculosis worldwide.

Economics

Jewish economists have also made significant contributions to the field of economics. Notably, John Harsanyi, John Nash, and Reinhard Selten were awarded the Nobel Prize in Economic Sciences in 1994 for their pioneering work in game theory. Their research revolutionized the understanding of strategic interactions between individuals and groups, with applications in various disciplines, including economics, politics, and psychology.

It is important to note that this section only scratches the surface of the many Jewish Nobel Prize laureates and scientific advancements. The Jewish community's influence and contributions in science have been vast and continue to shape our understanding of the world around us.

Example: Applications of Jewish Scientific Advancements

To further illustrate the impact of Jewish scientific advancements, let's consider an example of their application in medical research. Jewish Nobel laureate Paul Ehrlich's work on immunology and chemotherapy has paved the way for the development of targeted cancer therapies.

In modern oncology, researchers have built upon Ehrlich's concept of selectively targeting cancer cells while sparing healthy cells. By understanding the molecular mechanisms of different cancers, scientists can design drugs that specifically inhibit the growth and survival of cancer cells, leading to more effective and less toxic treatments.

For example, the development of Herceptin, a drug used in the treatment of HER2-positive breast cancer, is based on the understanding of specific cell surface receptors and their role in driving cancer growth. This targeted therapy has significantly improved survival rates and quality of life for patients with HER2-positive breast cancer.

The contributions of Jewish scientists and their groundbreaking research continue to impact various fields, improving our understanding of the world and transforming the way we approach scientific and medical challenges.

Summary

In this section, we highlighted the achievements of Jewish Nobel Prize laureates and their scientific advancements. From Albert Einstein's groundbreaking work on the Theory of Relativity to Paul Ehrlich's development of chemotherapy, the Jewish community's contributions to physics, chemistry, medicine, and economics have been influential and continue to shape scientific progress.

It is crucial to recognize and appreciate the contributions of individuals from diverse backgrounds in scientific endeavors, as their unique perspectives and experiences enrich our understanding of the world and drive innovation. The Jewish Nobel Prize laureates showcased in this section are just a few examples of the countless individuals who have made significant contributions to science and continue to inspire future generations of scientists.

Subsection 2: Jewish Contributions to Film, Music, and Literature

Jewish individuals have made exceptional contributions to the fields of film, music, and literature throughout history. Their unique perspectives, creativity, and storytelling abilities have enriched these art forms and left a lasting impact on global culture. In this subsection, we will explore some notable Jewish contributions and their influence on these artistic disciplines.

Film

The Jewish community has played a crucial role in shaping the film industry, both in front of and behind the camera. Jewish filmmakers have consistently pushed artistic boundaries, challenging social norms, and offering new narratives. Their work reflects their experiences of displacement, identity, and resilience.

One prominent Jewish filmmaker is Steven Spielberg, who has directed some of the most iconic films in cinematic history. His masterpiece "Schindler's List" (1993) brought the Holocaust to the forefront of public consciousness and won seven Academy Awards, including Best Picture and Best Director. The film serves as a powerful depiction of Jewish history and the human capacity for both cruelty and compassion.

Woody Allen, another notable Jewish filmmaker, has made significant contributions to the comedy genre. His unique blend of wit, neurotic characters, and complex storytelling has influenced generations of filmmakers. Movies like "Annie Hall" (1977) and "Manhattan" (1979) are prime examples of Allen's distinctive style and exploration of Jewish identity.

In recent years, Jewish filmmakers have continued to make an impact on the industry. Greta Gerwig, with films like "Lady Bird" (2017) and "Little Women" (2019), has brought fresh perspectives to coming-of-age stories. The Coen Brothers, known for their dark humor and intricate storytelling, have created celebrated films such as "Fargo" (1996) and "No Country for Old Men" (2007).

Music

Jewish musicians have made significant contributions to various genres of music, from classical compositions to contemporary popular music. Their music often reflects their cultural heritage, personal struggles, and social commentary.

Classical music has seen remarkable contributions from Jewish composers throughout history. Gustav Mahler, one of the most influential composers of the late Romantic period, created symphonies that delved into existential themes and explored the depths of human emotions. Felix Mendelssohn, a composer from the Romantic era, was known for his intricate melodies and harmonic innovations.

In the world of popular music, Jewish artists have had a profound impact. Bob Dylan, born Robert Zimmerman, revolutionized folk music with his poetic lyrics and politically charged songs. He became a voice for social activism and inspired countless musicians to use their art as a means of protest.

Similarly, Leonard Cohen's introspective songwriting and distinctive voice made him an iconic figure in the music industry. Songs like "Hallelujah" have become timeless classics, resonating with audiences around the world.

Contemporary Jewish musicians continue to shape the music landscape. Regina Spektor, known for her unique blend of pop and folk, infuses her songs with introspection and vulnerability. Adam Levine, the lead vocalist of Maroon 5, has achieved tremendous success with his band, producing chart-topping hits that have captivated audiences globally.

Literature

Jewish writers have made profound contributions to world literature, tackling a wide range of themes and genres. Their works often explore identity, memory, and the complexities of human existence.

Franz Kafka, a German-language writer of Jewish descent, is regarded as one of the most influential figures in modern literature. His complex narratives and existential themes in works like "The Metamorphosis" and "The Trial" have had a lasting impact on the literary world.

Saul Bellow, a Nobel Prize-winning author, explored themes of Jewish identity and American society in his novels. His works, including "The Adventures of Augie March" and "Herzog," showcase his ability to blend realism and social critique.

In contemporary literature, Jonathan Safran Foer has gained recognition for his novels that touch upon Jewish history and intergenerational trauma. His debut novel, "Everything Is Illuminated" (2002), intertwines historical fiction, magical realism, and personal narrative to explore the Holocaust and the complex fabric of Jewish identity.

Another notable Jewish writer is Philip Roth, whose works examine themes of American Jewish life and identity. His novel "American Pastoral" won the Pulitzer Prize for Fiction in 1998, depicting the challenges of assimilation and the American dream.

The Jewish community's contributions to film, music, and literature have left an enduring legacy. Their creativity, resilience, and ability to capture the complexities of the human experience continue to inspire and resonate with audiences worldwide.

Exercise: Think about a film, song, or book that has resonated with you on a personal level. Reflect on how it has influenced your perspectives or touched your emotions. Consider the themes and messages behind the work and how it might relate to the Jewish contributions discussed in this section.

Additional Resources:

- *The 50 Greatest Jewish Movies: A Critic's Ranking of the Very Best*, by Kathryn Bernheimer
- *The New Jews*, edited by Dan Opatoshu
- *Jewish American Literature: A Norton Anthology*, edited by Jules Chametzky, John Felstiner, Hilene Flanzbaum, and Kathryn Hellerstein

Trivia: Did you know that the first woman to win an Academy Award for Best Director was Jewish? Barbra Streisand received this honor in 1984 for her work on the film "Yentl," a story deeply rooted in Jewish culture and tradition.

Subsection 3: Jewish Philosophers and Thinkers

Jewish philosophers and thinkers have made profound contributions to the fields of philosophy, ethics, and theology throughout history. Their philosophical inquiries and intellectual insights have influenced not only Judaism but also had an impact on the broader Western intellectual tradition. In this subsection, we will explore some of the key figures and ideas in Jewish philosophy and their lasting relevance.

Philosophical Exploration of Existence

One of the central concerns of Jewish philosophers has been the exploration of the nature of existence and the meaning of life. Jewish philosophy seeks to understand the relationship between God, human beings, and the world, and how these entities interrelate.

One notable Jewish philosopher is Moses Maimonides (1138-1204), whose work "Guide for the Perplexed" delves into various philosophical topics, including the nature of God, the purpose of the Torah, and the concept of human intellect. Maimonides sought to reconcile Jewish religious belief with Aristotelian philosophy, emphasizing the role of reason and rationality in understanding divine truths.

Another important thinker is Baruch Spinoza (1632-1677), whose controversial works pushed the boundaries of traditional Jewish thought. Spinoza's philosophy, outlined in his masterpiece "Ethics," challenged traditional religious beliefs and emphasized a pantheistic view of God as nature or the universe. His ideas sparked debates within the Jewish community and influenced subsequent philosophical movements, such as Enlightenment rationalism.

Ethics and Morality

Jewish philosophers have also contributed extensively to the study of ethics and morality, providing insightful guidance on how people ought to live their lives and make ethical decisions.

One prominent Jewish philosopher in this area is Rabbi Moses ben Maimon, also known as Maimonides. In his book "Mishneh Torah," Maimonides outlines a comprehensive ethical framework based on Jewish law and teachings. He presents the concept of the "golden mean" in ethics, advocating for a balanced and virtuous approach to life, where one avoids extremes and cultivates virtues such as wisdom, humility, and benevolence.

Another notable figure is Martin Buber (1878-1965), whose philosophy of dialogue emphasized the importance of authentic relationship-building. Buber argued that true ethical living involves engaging in genuine dialogue, where individuals treat one another as unique subjects rather than objects. His work has had a profound influence on fields such as psychology, sociology, and interfaith dialogue.

Religion and Theology

Jewish philosophers have also grappled with fundamental questions about the nature of God, the purpose of religious practice, and the relationship between faith and reason.

Franz Rosenzweig (1886-1929) explored these themes in his work "The Star of Redemption." Rosenzweig emphasized the importance of religious experience and argued that faith is not merely a matter of intellectual affirmation but a transformative encounter with the divine. He also emphasized the significance of Jewish particularity within a broader universal context.

Another significant figure is Abraham Joshua Heschel (1907-1972), who addressed the relevance of spirituality in modern society. Heschel advocated for a experiential approach to religion, emphasizing the importance of awe, wonder, and reverence in encountering the divine. His writings have influenced contemporary Jewish theology and interfaith conversations.

Relevance and Contemporary Significance

The ideas put forth by Jewish philosophers and thinkers continue to have relevance and contemporary significance. Their inquiries into existence, ethics, and theology provide insightful frameworks for individuals grappling with questions of meaning and purpose in the modern world.

Moreover, Jewish philosophy's emphasis on reason and intellectual rigor serves as a testament to the compatibility of faith and reason, challenging the notion of an inherent conflict between religion and science. Jewish thinkers have often sought to reconcile religious belief with rationality, contributing to ongoing dialogue between scientific and religious worldviews.

It is through the works of Jewish philosophers and thinkers that we are invited to engage in deep reflection, expand our understanding of the world, and strive for ethical living. Their intellectual contributions continue to shape the rich cultural tapestry of Jewish thought and have a broader impact on the philosophical and theological landscape.

Subsection 4: Jewish Influence on Contemporary Culture

Jews have made significant contributions to contemporary culture, particularly in the fields of arts, entertainment, literature, and science. This section explores some of the key areas where Jewish individuals have had a profound impact on shaping the cultural landscape of the modern world.

Theater and Film

In the realm of theater and film, Jewish artists have played a pivotal role in revolutionizing storytelling, pushing boundaries, and challenging societal norms. One of the most notable figures in this regard is Steven Spielberg, the renowned filmmaker behind blockbuster movies such as "Jurassic Park," "Jaws," and "Schindler's List." Spielberg's films often explore themes of Jewish identity, history, and the human condition, captivating audiences worldwide.

Mel Brooks, another iconic Jewish figure in comedy, has left an indelible mark on both the stage and screen with his unique blend of satire and irreverence. From "The Producers" to "Young Frankenstein," Brooks has consistently pushed comedic boundaries, using humor to address social and cultural issues.

Literature and Philosophy

Jewish writers and thinkers have made significant contributions to literature and philosophy, enriching our understanding of the human experience. Saul Bellow, a Nobel laureate in Literature, wove together complex stories that explored the challenges of American Jewish identity. His works, including "Herzog" and "The Adventures of Augie March," continue to resonate with readers today.

The influence of Jewish philosophy can also be seen in the works of Martin Buber, a prominent Jewish theologian, and philosopher. Buber's groundbreaking concept of "I-Thou" relationships, which emphasizes the importance of genuine human connections, has had a profound impact on existentialist thought and interpersonal relationships.

Music and Art

Jewish musicians have made groundbreaking contributions to various genres of music. From classical to jazz and rock, their influence can be seen in the works of renowned composers and performers. Leonard Bernstein, a celebrated conductor and composer, showcased his talent through compositions like "West Side Story" and "Candide," bridging the gap between classical and popular music.

In the art world, Marc Chagall stands out as an influential Jewish figure. His vibrant and dreamlike paintings, often depicting Jewish themes and biblical stories, broke away from traditional artistic conventions. Chagall's art continues to inspire and captivate audiences worldwide.

Science and Technology

Jewish scientists and inventors have made groundbreaking contributions to various fields, advancing our understanding of the world and improving our daily lives. Albert Einstein, one of the greatest scientific minds of the 20th century, revolutionized physics with his theory of relativity. His work not only redefined our understanding of space, time, and gravity but also challenged prevailing scientific paradigms.

Further contributing to the field of science, Rosalind Franklin played a critical role in discovering the structure of DNA. Although her work was overshadowed at the time, her contributions were instrumental in unraveling the mysteries of life.

Contemporary Challenges and Jewish Perspectives

While Jewish individuals have made significant contributions to contemporary culture, it is important to acknowledge the challenges they face. Anti-Semitism persists in various forms, reminding us of the ongoing need to promote inclusivity, celebrate diversity, and challenge prejudice.

In conclusion, the Jewish influence on contemporary culture is undeniable. Jewish artists, writers, scientists, and thinkers have enriched our world with their creativity, intellect, and unique perspectives. By embracing and celebrating these contributions, we can foster a more inclusive and culturally diverse society.

Exercise: Reflect on the Jewish artists, writers, musicians, or scientists who have made an impact on contemporary culture. Choose one individual and write a short essay exploring their contributions and their impact on their respective field. Discuss how their Jewish identity influenced their work and the challenges they may have faced.

Section 2: Muslim Innovations and Influence on Civilization

Subsection 1: Muslim Scholars and Scientific Accomplishments

Muslim scholars have made significant contributions to various fields of science throughout history. These contributions have had a profound impact on the development of scientific knowledge and have shaped our understanding of the world. In this subsection, we will explore some of the major scientific accomplishments of Muslim scholars.

1. Islamic Golden Age: During the Islamic Golden Age, which lasted from the 8th to the 14th century, Muslim scholars made remarkable advancements in various disciplines, including mathematics, astronomy, physics, medicine, and chemistry. This period saw the translation and preservation of Greek, Roman, and Persian texts, as well as the development of new theories and ideas.

2. Mathematics: Muslim mathematicians significantly expanded upon the works of earlier civilizations and developed algebra and trigonometry as independent branches of mathematics. One of the most influential mathematicians of this time was Muhammad ibn Musa al-Khwarizmi, who introduced the concept of "algorithm" and laid the foundation for modern algebra. Other notable mathematicians include Al-Khwarizmi's student, Thabit ibn Qurra, and the Persian scholar Omar Khayyam.

3. Astronomy: Muslim astronomers made important contributions to the field of astronomy. They developed precise instruments, such as the astrolabe, for

celestial observations. One of the remarkable achievements was the work of Nasir al-Din al-Tusi, who proposed a new planetary model that explained the motion of celestial bodies. Al-Tusi's model served as the basis for later astronomers, including Nicolaus Copernicus.

4. Physics: Muslim scholars made significant advancements in the field of physics. The Persian polymath Ibn al-Haytham, known as Alhazen, is often regarded as the "Father of Optics." He wrote extensively on the nature of light and vision and conducted experiments to understand the principles of reflection and refraction. Alhazen's work laid the foundation for the modern scientific understanding of optics.

5. Medicine: Muslim physicians made significant contributions to the field of medicine, building on the knowledge of Greek, Roman, and Indian scholars. One prominent figure in Islamic medicine was Ibn Sina, commonly known as Avicenna. His book, "The Canon of Medicine," became a renowned medical encyclopedia and was widely used across Europe for centuries. Avicenna's work covered various aspects of medicine, including anatomy, physiology, and pharmacology.

6. Chemistry: Muslim scholars played a crucial role in the development of early chemistry. They conducted experiments and made discoveries in the fields of alchemy and chemical reactions. One notable figure was Jabir ibn Hayyan, known as Geber in the Western world. He worked extensively on distillation, purification, and developing various chemical apparatus. Geber's contributions laid the groundwork for future advancements in chemistry.

7. Preservation and Transmission of Knowledge: Muslim scholars played a vital role in preserving and translating ancient texts from Greek, Roman, and Persian civilizations. They established libraries and centers of learning, such as the House of Wisdom in Baghdad, where scholars from different cultures and backgrounds worked together to translate and study ancient texts. These translations and commentaries helped to preserve knowledge and fuel new discoveries.

The contributions of Muslim scholars to science and knowledge were not limited to these areas alone. Their work influenced and enriched various other disciplines, such as geography, engineering, architecture, and agriculture.

It is important to recognize and acknowledge the immense contributions of Muslim scholars throughout history. By embracing their legacy, we gain a deeper understanding of the interconnectedness of civilizations and the collective human quest for knowledge and understanding.

Example: The Quadratic Equation Invention

One fascinating example of the contributions of Muslim scholars to mathematics is the invention of the quadratic equation. The quadratic equation, commonly expressed as $ax^2 + bx + c = 0$, plays a fundamental role in algebra and has numerous practical applications.

The Persian mathematician Al-Khwarizmi, during the Islamic Golden Age, is credited with introducing the concept of the quadratic equation in his seminal work, "Al-Kitab al-Mukhtasar fi Hisab al-Jabr wa'l-Muqabala." In this book, Al-Khwarizmi explained the process of solving the quadratic equation using geometric methods.

Al-Khwarizmi's work was later translated into Latin during the 12th century, and his methods gained widespread recognition in Europe. His contributions laid the foundation for future advancements in algebra and made a lasting impact on the development of mathematics.

The quadratic equation is used in various fields, including physics, engineering, economics, and computer science. Its solutions provide critical insights into the behavior of complex systems and help solve real-world problems. The invention of the quadratic equation by Muslim scholars illustrates the immense practical significance of their contributions and the lasting impact of their work.

Exercise: Solving Quadratic Equations

1. Solve the following quadratic equation using the quadratic formula:

$$2x^2 - 7x + 3 = 0$$

2. A ball is thrown into the air with an initial velocity of 35 m/s. The height of the ball can be modeled by the quadratic equation $h(t) = -5t^2 + 35t + 1$, where t represents time in seconds and h represents the height in meters. Determine the time when the ball reaches its maximum height.

Additional Resources:

1. "The Genius of Islam: How Muslims Made the Modern World" by Bryn Barnard 2. "Muslim Scientists: Their Contributions to the Sciences" by S. Barrucand and A. Hamilton

Subsection 2: Islamic Art and Architecture

Islamic art and architecture are rich and diverse forms of artistic expression that have evolved over centuries within the Islamic world. This section will explore the key elements and characteristics of Islamic art and architecture, as well as their cultural significance and influences.

Historical Context

Islamic art and architecture have their roots in the religion of Islam, which emerged in the 7th century in the Arabian Peninsula. With its rapid expansion across the

Middle East, North Africa, and parts of Europe, Islamic art and architecture began to develop a distinct visual language that blended various cultural and artistic traditions.

Principles of Islamic Art

Islamic art is guided by several key principles that shape its visual aesthetic. These principles include:

1. *Calligraphy:* Calligraphy, or the art of beautiful writing, is one of the most prominent features of Islamic art. Arabic script, which is based on the Qur'an, is skillfully incorporated into various art forms, such as ceramics, textiles, and architecture.

2. *Geometric Patterns:* Islamic art frequently employs intricate geometric patterns, often based on a grid or tessellations. These patterns symbolize the infinite nature of God and are found in various art forms, such as tilework, carpets, and textiles.

3. *Floral and Vegetal Motifs:* Islamic art also incorporates floral and vegetal motifs, often depicted in a stylized and abstract manner. These motifs represent the natural world and can be found in architectural ornamentation, manuscript illumination, and textile design.

4. *Arabesque:* Arabesque is a decorative element characterized by flowing, intricate designs of scrolling foliage and tendrils. It is often combined with other artistic principles, such as calligraphy and geometric patterns, to create visually captivating compositions.

Architecture

Islamic architecture encompasses a wide range of structures, including mosques, palaces, tombs, and madrasas (educational institutions). Here are some notable features and elements of Islamic architecture:

1. *Mosque Architecture:* Mosques are central to Islamic religious and communal life. They typically feature a large prayer hall, a minaret (tower), and a qibla wall indicating the direction of Mecca. Islamic mosque architecture varies across regions, showcasing a fusion of local building traditions and Islamic influences.

2. *Domes and Arches:* Islamic architecture is known for its extensive use of domes and arches. Domes symbolize the celestial sphere and are often adorned with intricate geometric patterns or calligraphy. Arches, such as horseshoe, pointed, and multi-lobed arches, are found in both structural and decorative elements of Islamic buildings.

3. *Courtyards and Gardens:* Many Islamic architectural structures include spacious courtyards and gardens. These spaces serve both functional and symbolic purposes, providing natural ventilation, contemplative areas, and places for communal gatherings.

4. *Minarets:* Minarets are tall towers, often with a slender and cylindrical shape, attached to mosques. They serve as a visual marker for the mosque while also providing a platform for the call to prayer (adhan) by the muezzin.

Influence and Global Spread

Islamic art and architecture have had a profound influence on various artistic traditions around the world. Here are some examples of their influence:

1. *Moorish Architecture:* Islamic architectural styles had a significant impact on the development of Moorish architecture, which can be seen in the Alhambra in Granada, Spain, and the Great Mosque of Cordoba.

2. *Mughal Architecture:* Islamic architecture greatly influenced the opulent Mughal architecture of India, as seen in the Taj Mahal and the Red Fort in Delhi. Mughal architecture synthesized Islamic, Persian, and Indian elements to create unique structures.

3. *Ottoman Architecture:* Ottoman architecture drew inspiration from Byzantine, Roman, and Islamic architectural styles, resulting in iconic structures like the Hagia Sophia and the Sultan Ahmed Mosque (Blue Mosque) in Istanbul.

4. *Contemporary Islamic Art:* Islamic art continues to evolve and inspire contemporary artists worldwide, blending traditional elements with modern aesthetics. Artists like Shirin Neshat and Ahmed Mater explore themes of identity, culture, and spirituality in their works.

Contemporary Challenges and Preservation

Preserving Islamic art and architecture poses significant challenges due to factors like urbanization, conflicts, and changing societal attitudes. Efforts are being made to safeguard these cultural treasures through conservation initiatives, documentation, and raising awareness about their importance.

Conclusion

Islamic art and architecture reflect the rich cultural heritage and religious traditions of the Islamic world. They embody the principles of calligraphy, geometric patterns, and floral motifs, creating visually stunning and spiritually meaningful artworks. From mosques to palaces, their influence can be seen in architectural marvels across different regions. By understanding the significance and uniqueness of Islamic art and architecture, we can appreciate the contributions of Muslim communities to the global cultural landscape.

Subsection 3: Contributions to Medicine and Mathematics

In this subsection, we will explore the significant contributions that Muslim scholars have made to the fields of medicine and mathematics throughout history. These contributions, which emerged during the Islamic Golden Age, have had a lasting impact on the development of these disciplines and have paved the way for future advancements.

Medical Innovations

Muslim scholars in the medieval period made pioneering discoveries and advancements in the field of medicine. The renowned Muslim physician, Al-Razi, also known as Rhazes, made significant contributions to the understanding of various diseases and their treatment. He compiled an extensive medical encyclopedia, the "Kitab al-Hawi," which discussed numerous medical topics, including pediatrics, gynecology, and ophthalmology.

One of the most notable Muslim physicians of the time was Ibn Sina, commonly known as Avicenna. He wrote the influential medical encyclopedia, the "Canon of Medicine," which became a standard text in European medical education for centuries. Avicenna's work covered a wide range of medical topics, including anatomy, physiology, pharmacology, and surgery. He also developed new diagnostic methods and treatments for various diseases.

Muslim scholars also made significant contributions to the field of pharmacology. They studied and cataloged various medicinal plants and herbs, contributing to a better understanding of their therapeutic properties. Additionally, Muslim physicians developed innovative pharmaceutical techniques, such as distillation and extraction, to produce more effective medications.

Example: Unani Medicine Unani medicine, also known as Graeco-Arabic medicine, is a traditional healing system that originated from the teachings of Hippocrates and Galen, enriched by Islamic medical knowledge. Unani medicine integrates elements from Greek, Roman, and Arabic medical traditions and continues to be practiced in many parts of the world, particularly in South Asia.

Unani medicine emphasizes the harmony between the body, mind, and spirit in maintaining health. It employs a holistic approach to diagnosis and treatment, considering multiple factors such as lifestyle, diet, and environmental influences. Unani practitioners utilize a wide range of remedies, including herbal medicines, dietary interventions, cupping (a form of therapy), and massage.

Mathematical Contributions

Muslim mathematicians during the Islamic Golden Age contributed significantly to the development of various mathematical fields, including algebra, trigonometry, and number theory. Their work not only preserved and expanded upon ancient knowledge but also introduced groundbreaking concepts and techniques.

One of the most influential Muslim mathematicians was Muhammad al-Khwarizmi, who is often referred to as the "Father of Algebra." His book, "Kitab al-Jabr wa al-Muqabala" (The Compendious Book on Calculation by Completion and Balancing), laid the foundations for modern algebra. Al-Khwarizmi introduced systematic methods for solving linear and quadratic equations, including the use of variables and manipulating mathematical expressions.

Another notable mathematician, Al-Biruni, made significant contributions to trigonometry. He developed methods to calculate trigonometric functions and used them to accurately determine the Earth's radius. His work laid the foundation for modern trigonometric concepts and was later built upon by European mathematicians.

Example: Algebraic Geometry Algebraic geometry, a branch of mathematics that combines algebra and geometry, owes much to the contributions of Muslim mathematicians. Their work on algebra and geometric concepts formed the basis for the development of this field.

Algebraic geometry studies the relationships between algebraic equations and geometric shapes. It involves techniques such as converting geometric problems into algebraic equations and using algebraic methods to solve geometric problems. This field finds applications in various areas, including computer science, cryptography, and physics.

Summary

Muslim scholars have left a lasting impact on medicine and mathematics through their pioneering discoveries and advancements. Their contributions have enriched our understanding of various diseases, treatment methods, and pharmaceutical techniques in the field of medicine. In mathematics, they developed revolutionary concepts and techniques that laid the foundation for algebra, trigonometry, and other mathematical disciplines. The work of these scholars continues to inspire and guide researchers in these areas, emphasizing the timeless significance of their contributions.

Key Takeaways

- Muslim scholars during the Islamic Golden Age made significant contributions to the fields of medicine and mathematics.
- Muslim physicians like Al-Razi and Ibn Sina advanced medical knowledge through their comprehensive encyclopedias.
- Unani medicine is an example of a traditional healing system that integrates Greek, Roman, and Arabic medical traditions.
- Muslim mathematicians, such as al-Khwarizmi and Al-Biruni, played crucial roles in the development of algebra, trigonometry, and other mathematical disciplines.
- Algebraic geometry emerged from the combined efforts of Muslim mathematicians in algebra and geometry.

Further Reading

For further exploration of the contributions of Muslim scholars in medicine and mathematics, the following resources are recommended:

1. Ahmed, S. Z. (1984). Science in Islam: A Historical Perspective. Taylor & Francis.

2. Dallal, A. (2010). Islam, Science, and the Challenge of History. Yale University Press.

3. Hogendijk, J., & Sabra, A. I. (Eds.). (2010). The Enterprise of Science in Islam: New Perspectives. The MIT Press.

4. Saidan, A. S. (1983). Islamic Medicine: History and Current Practice. Routledge.

These resources provide in-depth insights into the contributions of Muslim scholars and the historical context in which they emerged. They offer a comprehensive understanding of the achievements made by Muslim scholars in medicine and mathematics and their ongoing relevance in modern times.

Subsection 4: Islamic Influence on Literature and Poetry

In this subsection, we will explore the profound influence of Islamic culture on literature and poetry. Islamic civilization has a rich literary tradition that spans over centuries, encompassing a wide range of genres and themes. From the early days of Islam to the modern age, Islamic literature and poetry have played a vital role in shaping the cultural landscape of the Islamic world and beyond.

Historical Background

To understand the influence of Islamic literature and poetry, it is essential to delve into the historical context in which these art forms developed. With the spread of Islam in the 7th century, a new intellectual, artistic, and literary tradition emerged in the Arab world. The Quran, the holy book of Islam, served as a primary source of inspiration for literary and poetic expressions.

During the Islamic Golden Age (8th to 14th centuries), scholars translated and preserved ancient Greek, Persian, and Indian texts, leading to a flourishing of knowledge and creativity. This period witnessed an immense growth in Islamic literature, with poets, scholars, and philosophers producing works of exceptional beauty and intellectual depth.

Characteristics of Islamic Literature and Poetry

Islamic literature and poetry are characterized by several distinctive features that set them apart from other literary traditions. These features include:

1. The Power of Language: Islamic literature emphasizes the eloquence and power of language. Arabic, the language of the Quran, became the dominant

language of Islamic literature. Arabic poetry, renowned for its complex rhyme schemes and meter, became a highly regarded art form.

2. Themes of Love, Spirituality, and Morality: Islamic literature and poetry often explore themes of love, spirituality, and morality. Poets expressed their devotion to God, the Prophet Muhammad, and their love for humanity through poetry. Sufi poetry, in particular, delved into mystical experiences and the longing for spiritual union with the divine.

3. Rich Symbolism and Imagery: Islamic poetry is known for its vivid imagery and rich symbolism. Poets often used metaphors, allegories, and symbols to convey deeper meanings, creating a profound aesthetic experience for the reader or listener.

4. Oral Tradition and Performance: Islamic poetry has a strong oral tradition, with poets reciting their work in public gatherings or in the courts of rulers. The rhythmic and melodic qualities of Arabic poetry enhance the performance aspect, captivating audiences through the power of spoken word.

Major Works and Authors

Throughout history, numerous Islamic poets and writers have left an indelible mark on the literary world. Some of the most renowned works and authors include:

1. Rumi: Jalal ad-Din Muhammad Rumi, a 13th-century Persian poet, is celebrated for his mystical poems that explore love, spirituality, and the quest for truth. His masterpiece, the Mathnawi, remains one of the most influential works of Persian literature.

2. Al-Mutanabbi: Abu al-Tayyib Ahmad ibn al-Husayn al-Mutanabbi, an Arab poet of the 10th century, is considered one of the greatest classical Arabic poets. Known for his eloquence and mastery of the Arabic language, Al-Mutanabbi's poems reflect themes of heroism, power, and social critique.

3. Ibn Arabi: Muhyiddin ibn Arabi, a 12th-century Andalusian philosopher, theologian, and poet, is recognized as one of the most important figures in Sufi literature. His works, such as the Fusus al-Hikam and Tarjuman al-Ashwaq, explore profound spiritual insights and metaphysical concepts.

4. Nizar Qabbani: Nizar Qabbani, a 20th-century Syrian poet, contributed to the revival of Arabic poetry in the modern era. His poems, often focused on themes of love, feminism, and Arab nationalism, have resonated with readers throughout the Arab world.

Islamic Literature and Poetry in Different Regions

Islamic literature and poetry have flourished in various regions influenced by Islamic culture. Here, we highlight a few notable examples:

1. Persian Literature: Persian literature has a rich tradition dating back to the medieval period. Influenced by both Islamic and pre-Islamic traditions, Persian poets such as Omar Khayyam and Hafez have crafted exquisite verses of love, mysticism, and philosophical contemplation.
2. Urdu Poetry: Urdu, a language developed in Northern India during the Mughal Empire, became a vehicle for expressing Islamic themes through poetry. Notable Urdu poets like Mirza Ghalib and Allama Iqbal explored the intricacies of love, faith, and social justice in their verses.
3. Andalusian Poetry: During the Islamic rule in Andalusia (modern-day Spain and Portugal), a vibrant culture of poetry thrived. Poets like Ibn Zaydun and Wallada bint al-Mustakfi embraced themes of love, nostalgia, and societal complexities in their compositions.

Contemporary Influences

Islamic literature and poetry continue to inspire contemporary authors and poets worldwide. Modern writers of Islamic heritage, such as Khaled Hosseini, Leila Aboulela, and Mohja Kahf, explore diverse themes and approaches while drawing on Islamic literary traditions.

In addition to the direct influence on literature, Islamic poetry has also infiltrated popular culture. Artists, musicians, and performers frequently draw inspiration from Islamic poetry, infusing it into their creative expressions. Islamic motifs and symbolism have found their way into contemporary art, music, and fashion, creating a unique fusion of ancient traditions and modern sensibilities.

Conclusion

The Islamic influence on literature and poetry is a testament to the richness and complexity of Islamic civilization. From the eloquence of the Quran to the poetic expressions of love and spirituality, Islamic literature and poetry have left an indelible mark on the literary world. By exploring this influence, we gain a deeper understanding of the cultural heritage and intellectual contributions of the Islamic world. Islamic literature and poetry continue to captivate readers and serve as a source of inspiration for contemporary artists and writers, ensuring that this rich tradition endures for generations to come.

As you immerse yourself in the world of Islamic literature and poetry, take time to reflect on the beauty of language, the universality of themes, and the profound impact these works have had on the intellectual and artistic trajectory of humanity.

Subsection 5: Muslim Contributions to Philosophy and Ethics

Muslim scholars throughout history have made significant contributions to the fields of philosophy and ethics. From the early Islamic Golden Age to the present day, Muslim thinkers have tackled profound questions about the nature of reality, the purpose of human existence, and the principles that govern moral behavior. In this section, we will explore some of the key contributions made by Muslim philosophers and ethicists, as well as their lasting impact on intellectual thought.

Background and Development of Islamic Philosophy

Islamic philosophy emerged in the 8th century CE, drawing inspiration from various intellectual traditions, including Greek, Persian, and Indian philosophy. Muslim philosophers sought to reconcile reason and rational inquiry with Islamic theology and scripture, creating a rich and diverse intellectual tradition.

One of the major figures in the development of Islamic philosophy was Al-Kindi (9th century CE). He emphasized the compatibility between philosophy and Islam, arguing that rational inquiry can be a tool to understand and appreciate God's creation.

Another key figure was Al-Farabi (10th century CE), known as the "Second Teacher" after Aristotle, he made significant contributions to political philosophy and ethics. He emphasized the importance of cultivating virtuous individuals and just societies.

Metaphysics and Epistemology

Muslim philosophers delved into questions of metaphysics and epistemology, exploring the nature of reality and the limits of human knowledge. One notable philosopher in this realm is Ibn Sina (Avicenna), whose work greatly influenced both Islamic and Western philosophy.

Ibn Sina developed a comprehensive metaphysical system based on his concept of "necessary existence." He argued for the existence of a necessary being, which he identified as God, and explored various cosmological arguments for God's existence.

In the realm of epistemology, Ibn Sina formulated a theory of knowledge that distinguished between "knowledge by presence" and "knowledge by representation." He emphasized the importance of reason and rational inquiry, while also acknowledging the limitations of human understanding.

Ethics and Moral Philosophy

Muslim philosophers made significant contributions to the field of ethics, grappling with questions of moral responsibility, ethical values, and the nature of good and evil.

One influential Muslim ethicist was Al-Ghazali (11th century CE), who emphasized the importance of moral conduct and the purification of the soul. He argued that true ethical transformation requires not only intellectual understanding but also a spiritual awakening.

Another notable figure was Ibn Rushd (Averroes), who championed the compatibility of reason and faith. He defended the use of rationality in moral decision-making and argued for the autonomy of ethics from religious authority.

Muslim ethicists also made contributions to applied ethics, including medical ethics and business ethics. For example, Ibn Sina discussed ethical considerations in medicine, such as the duty of physicians to prioritize the well-being of their patients.

Islamic Philosophy and Global Intellectual Thought

The contributions of Muslim philosophers and ethicists have had a profound impact on global intellectual thought. Their works were often translated into Latin during the medieval period, becoming instrumental in the development of Western philosophy.

One example is the influence of Ibn Rushd on Christian Scholasticism. His commentaries on Aristotle's works shaped the intellectual landscape of Europe and contributed to the revival of interest in Aristotelian philosophy.

Islamic philosophy also had a significant impact on Jewish intellectual thought. Jewish philosophers, such as Maimonides, engaged with and built upon the ideas of Muslim thinkers, leading to a rich exchange of ideas and the development of Judeo-Islamic philosophy.

Contemporary Relevance and Challenges

Today, Muslim philosophers and ethicists continue to contribute to the ongoing exploration of philosophy and ethics. They engage with contemporary issues such as social justice, environmental ethics, and the role of religion in ethical decision-making.

However, Islamic philosophy faces certain challenges in the modern world. Some contemporary scholars argue for a more contextual approach, integrating Islamic ethical values into broader global discourses. They seek to bridge the gap between tradition and modernity while also addressing the challenges of a rapidly changing world.

Furthermore, there is a need for increased recognition and engagement with diverse voices within the Muslim philosophical tradition, including those of women and marginalized communities. Efforts are being made to highlight the contributions of Muslim women philosophers and ethicists throughout history and to create inclusive spaces for dialogue and intellectual exchange.

In conclusion, Muslim philosophers and ethicists have made significant contributions to the fields of philosophy and ethics, shaping intellectual discourse both within and beyond the Islamic tradition. By exploring profound questions about the nature of reality and the principles guiding human behavior, they have enriched global intellectual thought and continue to inspire contemporary scholars in their ongoing pursuit of knowledge and wisdom.

Index

Printed by
Libri Plureos GmbH · Friedensallee 273
22763 Hamburg · Germany

9 781779 613530